Bryan Foster

Jesus and Mahomad are GOD

Bryan Foster

Jesus and Mahomad are GOD

(Author Articles)

Bryan Foster

Book Five of the 'GOD Today' Series

Bryan Foster

Published in 2020

Great Developments Publishers
(Bryan Foster and Karen Foster, Directors)
Gold Coast, Queensland, Australia 4217
ABN: 13133435168 USA-EIN: 98-0689457

All rights reserved. No part of this publication may be reproduced, stored in a retrieval system, transmitted in any forms or by any means, electronic, mechanical, photocopying, recording, or otherwise, without the prior permission of the publisher and copyright holders. The author and publisher disclaim liability for any use, misuse, misunderstanding of any information contained herein, or for any loss, damage or injury (be it health, financial or otherwise) for any individual or group acting upon or relying on information contained or inferred from this work.

The moral rights of the author have been asserted.

Copyright © Great Developments Publishers, 2020.

Creator: Foster, Bryan – author, publishing director

Title: Jesus and Mahomad are GOD

 A catalogue record for this book is available from the National Library of Australia

ISBN: 9780648400165 (hardback)
ISBN: 9780648400158 (paperback)
ISBN: 9780648400141 (ebook)
ISBN: 9780980610789 (large print paperback)

Notes: Includes bibliographical references and index.

'GOD Today' Series (2016-2021/2)

Published

1God.world: One God for All (Author Articles) (2016)

Mt Warning God's Revelations: Photobook Companion to '1God.world' (2017)

Where's God? Revelations Today (Author Articles) (2018)

Where's God? Revelations Today Photobook Companion: GOD Signs (2nd ed) (2018)

GOD Today Video Series (2018)

Jesus and Mahomad* are God (Author Articles) (2020)

*N.B. The spelling of 'Mahomad' is deliberate. It is as given by God to the author.

Published Soon

Love is the Meaning of Life: GOD'S Love (Articles) (2020)

Love is the Meaning of Life: GOD'S Love Photobook

Companion (2021/2)
Love is the Meaning of Life (Author Articles) (1st ed) (2020/1) (An introduction of God's Love to non-religious people)
Wisdom Made Real: A Lifetime of Godly Hints and Tips for Us All (Author Articles) (appr. 2021/2) (Working Title)

Websites

https://www.godtodayseries.com/
https://jesusandmahomadaregod.com/
https://www.bryanfosterauthor.com/
https://www.facebook.com/groups/389602698051426/

'GOD Today' Series' cover images and photobooks

Bryan Foster and Karen Foster, GDP.
Outstanding images from Andrew Foster (Austographer.com) from Australia now living in Canada.

Cover photo: Spectacularly unique, sunrise Gold Coast, Australia by Bryan Foster
Graphics: Bryan Foster and Bookpod

Dedication

Dedicated to Karen, the Love of my life, my wife of 42 years. My angel. My rock, my Uluru, my heart of Australia.
And to my loving children Leigh-Maree, Andrew, Jacqueline and daughter-in-law Shannon, son-in-law Matthew, grandchildren Kyan, Cruze, Felicity, Isabella, Max and Lyla.
To my parents, Frank (Deceased 2018) and Mary.
And to my siblings John, Susy and Clare and all my extended family.
Thank you for all your Love, support and encouragement.
To my dear friends and former colleagues over 42 years of teaching, thank you.

CONTENTS

Dedication	12
Contents	13
Foreword by Karen Foster	21
Special Invitation from Author	24
Overview	25
The Author's Call	25
'Will you be a Prophet?'	29
Atheists & Agnostics	33
Preview by key religions	34
Evidence of the Truth	35
It's God's Time!	37
Key New Revelations from God	38
21 Revelations from God – 2016 and 2018	45
God's Sun Signs Attract Us	46
Finding the Truth	47

Essential Appendices to Assist Stand-Alone Book	49
'Tears from God'	52
'God Today' Series Books' Release Dates	53
Two Incarnations of God – Jesus and Mahomad*	53
Stand Alone Book 5	55
No Illegitimate Violence Allowed by God	57
Faithful Challenged	60

*** (NB. The spelling of 'Mahomad' is deliberate. It is as told by God to the author.)

'GOD Today' Series	61
'GOD Today' Series - Overviews	63

INTRODUCTION 71

Suggested Sections and Articles for the Reader – depending on this *Series'* books previously read	86
It is God's Time	89
Revelation #15 – Jesus and Mahomad* are GOD	90

AUTHOR

Author by Karen Foster	97
Overview of Author's Lifetime Events Leading to the *'GOD Today' Series* – (see Appendix 4 – p.278)	
Author's Websites	102
"I am a Prophet Prophets are True"	103
Keep It Simple - KIS	104

TRUTHS

Are the Revelations and Inspired Messages contained in this Book the Truth from God?	110
Tears from God	124
Is the Author a Prophet? (Included with Revelations from God, 2016)	133
God's Prophet Question of the Author	140
So am I a Prophet?	145
COVID-19 Costs and Military Costs	149

Jesus and Mahomad* are GOD
ONE GOD - TWO INCARNATIONS

One God - Two Incarnations Overview	157
One God	159
One God - Two Incarnations	162
How on Earth could this be possible?	167

The Time is Now! We are all in this together	170
Our Response to God	173
God Directs Us	175
Science and Technology – God's Gifts	177
Revelation #15 – the Detail - Jesus & Mahomad are God	181
World, it is time to face reality!!!	188
Be as Positive as You Can	191
God Calls Religious Leaders to Act	195
God calls us to follow 'Him'	200

21 REVELATIONS FOR TODAY

God's Revelations #1-21	205
Latest Revelations (Nov 2018) #16-21 explained (Received from God after the publication of Book 4)	208

#16 We need God   209

#17 We need <u>to be Vulnerable to God</u>   212

#18 We need to be asking for God's help continually and assistance & support always. 'No big heads' - Just ask for help. Always.   215

#19 We are insignificant compared to God.   219

#20 God is so superior - face up to it. Believe it! Stop fighting it!   223

#21 Be meek & humble & real for God   227

Renumbering Revelations

#6. Die for what is right   231

#13. Cyberbullying – in all its forms, of all sorts of all ages   242

#14. Fear rules – often from the cyberworld - eliminate this   247

CONCLUSION 254

ESSENTIAL BACKGROUND

Appendix 1 - Revelations and Inspired Messages from God to the author (2016)   265

Appendix 2 - Mt Warning - Word of God Revelations, Early Morning 29, May 2016 - the Story (2016)   272

Appendix 3 - Inspired Messages - Afternoon of 28 May, 2016 (2018)   277

Appendix 4 - Author's Personal Life Events Leading to 'GOD Today' Series (2020)   278

Appendix 5 - Where it all began - Author's 25th Birthday (1982)   292

Appendix 6 - *1God.world: One God for All*, (2016) - Contents   300

Appendix 7 - *Where's God? Revelations Today* (2018) - Contents   307

Appendix 8 - '*Where's God? Revelations Today Photobook Companion: GOD Signs (2nd ed)*' (2018) – Contents   314

Appendix 9 - *Love is the Meaning of Life: GOD'S Love* (released 2020/1) - Contents (Draft)   316

Appendix 10 - Islam, Christianity, Secularism - Today's Challenges (2020)   318

Appendix 11 - 'OMG', 'O My God!' Little Respect for God?   327

Appendix 12 – Atheists & Agnostics (cont. from p.33)   331

Bibliography   **334**
Bibliographic References' Variation   **339**
Index   **343**
Author's Websites   **346**
Series Books' Release Dates   **347**
Publisher   **350**
Books by Author   **352**

Foreword by Karen Foster

I have witnessed God working through Bryan first-hand for many years as he helps others to find God personally in their lives. You are invited to explore these affirming messages from God for Today's world.

Jesus and Mahomad are God (2020) is the most challenging, yet inspirational Revelation from God! For this to have proper credibility, Bryan has included several reasons why these are the Truth from God, to be heard across the world. He relates many explanations throughout to support that these Revelations are from God. Readers of previous books in this *'God Today' Series* will notice references that help with the depth of these challenging Revelations from God.

1God.world: One God for All (2016) and *Where's God? Revelations Today (2018)* and *Where's God? Revelations Today Photobook Companion: GOD's Signs (2018)* invited us to join in the discovery of God, God's Revelations, and God's inspired messages as we strive to find our own personal and communal salvation with God. Being aware of coincidences and signs from God to people, including us, help direct our journey to God and Heaven.

The use of photographic signs, as shown in the photobook, *Where's God? Revelations Today Photobook Companion: GOD's Love (2018)*, are in themed sets of sun images that Bryan took. This unique approach helps to encourage the reader to search for God's intimacy in their own lives. We can then start seeing more of God and God's actions in our everyday world. This is us becoming one with God on Earth and leads to a higher level of 'Heaven' on Earth, guiding us to how we approach our lives to be pure of heart and mind at our death. Heaven, God and us together after death, is still an unknown existence for our discovery, but...? Why wait for death and arrival in Heaven? We can experience examples of 'Heaven on Earth' when we are very close to God, through prayer and a genuine loving lifestyle with God that leads to positive, loving relationships with people.

The fifth Book in Bryan's *'GOD Today' Series* – continues the journey of discovering God's Love that began with *1God.world: One God for All* and *Where's God? Revelations Today,* along with each Book's photobook companion. Bryan renews and continues further the exploration of who God is, what Love is, and how God can be discovered and followed. He builds on the twenty-six personal stories of the spiritual discovery of God in Book 1 and the twelve Revelations from God in Book 3.

Interestingly, because of the uniqueness and the challenge of the images in Book 4, these God creative images inspire us to be challenged to believe the Revelations do come directly from God. It is God doing what God does – no force or cohesion exerted. When you view Book Four, *'Where's God? Revelations Today Photobook Companion: GOD's Signs'* (2018) you will see magnificent and very different, unique images from God to us all. Bryan believes that this is *God trying to entice us to go that much further with 'His' Revelations. It is something like – you love these unique and challenging photos, now love all the Revelations and messages too!!!*

Bryan's next two books in this *Series* are to be released within the year. *Love is the Meaning of Life: GOD'S Love* and its photobook companion, show us how God's Love is at the forefront of everything we do.

(Karen and Bryan - married for 42 years.)

Special Invitation

Just as this book takes a very positive approach to all the claims made here about God and from God, as well as in all previous books in this *Series*, you are invited to approach it with a positivity that will help enhance your and our relationships and faith with God. All comments, whether emailed or on social media platforms etc., must be supportive of this approach. Negativity is not permitted on the author's websites and will be removed. Negativity and hate have dominated our world for way too long now and look how these have failed us.

It is GOD's turn NOW – WE LISTEN!!!

Overview

This next Book in the *'GOD Today' Series - Jesus and Mahomad are GOD (2020),* contains some of the most extraordinary Revelations from God for all of Today's people. Four key Revelations in this fifth Book will challenge at least three major beliefs of the two largest world religions, Christianity and Islam.

It is time, revealed God!

This overview is designed to bring the reader to a good starting point, as the author shares some vital information right here at the Book's beginning. These are then developed considerably throughout the text - often under different headings or themes but deliberately set to link with the topic being explored at that moment.

The Author's Call

So much has happened to me these past five years since the start of creating the *'GOD Today'*

Series! Various discoveries or presentations by or to me, but most commonly from God, have had significant impacts on the readers and myself.

For clarity, some crucial points are worth noting. I have not seen God directly. But, like many others, *I 'see' God everywhere*, e.g., in nature, communities, sacred places, and holy people, religious rituals and liturgies, in the people I love, my wife Karen, our children and grandchildren, parents and family, etc. Also, people who have been harmed or injured or ill. In social justice being alive and adding so much depth to people's lives, etc.

Yet, *I have heard God several times*. How? These mainly come through your thoughts, prayers, or meditations. It mostly happens when your beliefs, actions, celebrations, etc. are very close to God. The two sets of Revelations being explained in this Book 5 occurred during the early morning hours. God also uses the 'Tears from God', along with various worldly signs to help, primarily through multiple sun photographs for me these past few years.

This shows how almost every day, something will religiously inspire and possibly challenge us in a necessary divine encounter. Too many times, too many people ignore, deny, or even miss the experience that God had just given them. Be open to explore what might be, or is, God's presence in your lives.

Many people find that being open to anything divine, supernatural, or spiritual becomes an invitation to God to come to them. I certainly agree, mostly due to my experiences. As their experiences grow more frequently with God over time, they will learn so much about God and us. Each person will start to become much more Godlike, e.g., being open to God's Love and God's Truth, prayer, meditation, forgiveness, compassion, empathy, and justice, etc. and living and exemplifying God's Love for all of creation.

These are characteristics/descriptors of God and from God for each of us! It is how we are 'made in the image of God' – this belief gets quite confused at times. We freely gain the Godly qualities of God, not God's looks, because God is divine and not physical. Hence no looks from our human perspective!

The one exceptional reality, which I am incredibly humbled by and freely and honourably accept from God, has been the real, genuine Revelations and Inspired Messages received. These have become very frequent through the course of writing these books, now in the fifth year.

The questions most commonly asked are, how do I get the Revelations from God? Does God talk to me? There are a few ways that this happens. However, the last 21 Revelations in 2016 and 2018 were received in the early morning hours around 3 am. This means I was awoken. Both times I was camping in a caravan/trailer at two different venues on the plains, or the foot, of Mt Warning, NSW, Australia.

Once awake, I received the messages from God in my mind. How? It is sort of like becoming part of my thoughts - yet not being my thoughts. If aware, you actually know the difference too. In 2016 I was even told to, 'Don't overthink what's happening, just write it down.' And so I did, these were the 15 Revelations from May, 2016. I usually get the 'Tears from God' as one form of proof, yet not this time. It wasn't to happen until the next day at a First Communion Mass in the local church where Karen and I were married. I asked God if the last night's 15 Revelations were real, and the answer was obviously, 'Yes!' I received these very tearful, 'Tears from God' during the Eucharistic celebration. (Tears from God p.52ff, 124ff)

The 2018 Revelations were on a different camping ground, this time at the foot of Mt Warning. Yet, these were told by God and received by me in the same way as it was 2.5 years previous. These six are numbered from #16 to #21.

"Will you be a Prophet for Me?"

On top of these Revelations, I was asked by God to do something exceptional and very different from the norm. God's query of me was also received in the presence of my wife, Karen. It was the most humbling and enlightening experience I have ever had. I was asked to be a prophet and espouse these latest Revelations to the world. Wow! What can you say?

Even though we have Free Will and the genuine right to accept or reject God's offers, how could you reject it??? It was the most astounding offer - a most humbling, rewarding, and exciting moment from God. There were much apprehension and doubt with which to start. But over time, it began to become real and be seen as what I should do – but could I really do it?

I have a reasonable idea of how most people will respond to this. Being an Australian, living in Australia, you know that cutting the perceived 'tall poppies' down, is for some a daily challenge and an opportunity for so many!!! I would anticipate the possible loss of a few friends and colleagues over this. Also, being a religious book, many people worldwide will come out of the social media networks to humiliate me and these God-given beliefs. But they may not do so either!

So am I a prophet? I still don't fully know! See further discussion in this book under its heading.

Atheists and Agnostics – Search for God Called for…!

After all, as far as so many of these atheists and harmful others are concerned, I'm wasting space just thinking of publishing this Book 5. Totally truthless for them - being non-believers or rejectors. However, *I am hoping that you and I may start a spark, a light, somehow for them to search in ways they hadn't known before.* Eventually, the desire would be knowing that God is incredibly special and needs to be seen as very rewarding and loving for these folk.

Hopefully, this Book 5 will give people much to think about in their growth towards and with God. For this to work correctly, people usually need to be open, loving, and forgiving. As well as prepared to sometimes risk-take, often beyond their expectations.

With the uppermost respect and Love of God and all humanity, and *the need for humanity to believe in God individually, communally, BUT unquestionably*, I would like to add, "Atheists and agnostics, you must search for a real, authentically precious life filled with God's Love!!! Learn. Grow. Improve. Be Open. *Live God's Love/Live Love*!!! Seek forgiveness. Be forgiven.

God is real, no matter what you say, believe or teach, etc." Do you really want to take the rejection of God risk and not choose God at your death?

With so many Revelations, Signs from God, Inspired Messages, etc., as explained and built upon throughout the book, I would thoroughly hope that you could engage in some fruitful discussion for the world to grow and become as much as possible, a most God-loving, people-loving, peaceful place forever.

My most memorable experience of sharing some religious thoughts on social media was received exceptionally harshly, disrespectfully, and cruelly. These mostly professed non-believers and rejectors were quite spiteful and basically evil – everything against a belief in God was their aim for themselves and everyone else. Vindictive responses were ultimately hate-filled – EVIL!

Rejectors

These rejectors of God's reality are trying to convince believers – that this rejection itself is not evil, i.e., *rejecting God outright and forcefully is being evil personified. However, it is the rejection of God, not the unbelieving of God, which is evil.*

You have to know about God and then reject God to be a rejector.

When your deliberate, hurtful attack/arguments dominate, mainly due to your atheistic vilification of God and God's believers, atheists' evil actions and beliefs enter the world, and they try to convert the non-atheists to atheism, from good to evil. Yet, the opposite is in the believers' minds.

GOD IS REAL NO MATTER WHAT!!!

(Continued at - Appendix 12, p.331ff)

Preview by key religions

A common question often arises regarding any invitation I may have sent to Judaic-Christian and Islamic leaders to read this Book or question me about its Revelatory contents, uniqueness, and place in Today's world, etc. Also, how does it stack up against conventional beliefs and teachings of each religion, Christianity, and Islam, already? As well as, how do I know it is the actual Truth from God?!

I have thought about these options long and hard. In the long run, my decision has been not to engage with these religious leaders or scholars at this stage. There is no communication from God requesting that I do so. I think that if I did share these four Revelations at this stage pre-publication with various religious groups, religions, etc., their response could be to try and shut this down as quickly as possible. Probably, due to their lack of appreciation for my genuine evidence. The Truth of God's Revelations must prevail. That is this Book's primary purpose.

Yet, in all Truth, and appreciation of my religious study to Master's level, senior school teaching religion over 42 years, writing books and articles, plus the Revelations to me directly from God in 1982, 2016 and 2018, and my lifetime of reflecting, praying, meditating and discussing with others like-minded or against, etc. shows the necessary legitimacy. I will most likely, provide critical groups in both Christianity and Islam copies once released.

Evidence of the Truth

Another could be a challenge that there is no evidence of my accuracy and truthfulness - which is so incorrect! Whatever could challenge this accuracy when we accept that the principal, primary source, is GOD! It would come mainly through the Revelations and inspired messages, and sun signs shared with me, and I would imagine many others worldwide.

It is also where I would show accuracy based on:

- my receival of Revelations from God predominantly in 1981, 2016, and 2018. Plus numerous Inspired Messages and Discerned Messages over the years;
- the regularly experienced Tears from God since my 25th birthday experience. These are not emotional tears but something very unique when in a Loving relationship with God;
- the genuinely, acquired, physical, photographic images of sun arrows, rays, flares, and rainbows, etc. (see Photobook 4, my favourite image book in this *Series* for numerous photos, or view the GodTodaySeries.com website for a sample of images);
- the authentic, prophetic invitation from God, while with Karen on a particular evening last year, in addition to the prophetic claim written from God on the Revelations two-page record from 2018, etc.

All this comes from the genuine Revelations from God, as the primary source of much of my evidence.

It's God's Time

It is now that moment in history when Islam and Christianity need to listen to God through these latest and incredibly supportive Revelations necessary in Today's world. I believe that God should, in no way, be diminished in the reader's eyes through this occurrence. *The Incarnations of God may not be limited to Jesus and Mahomad,* nor are the two specific religions diminished in any way, shape, or form. Time will tell. All should be very much strengthened.

What these Revelations aim to achieve is to open the minds and attitudes of people seeking the Truth from God for humanity Today. It is not acceptable to cling onto or reject everything of the past as our world continually changes over the centuries and millennia. Yes, most critical aspects of these religions won't change, but some will, as explained in this Book.

Revelations #6 and #15 revealed in 2016 are explored for the first time in this Book 5. These are two considerable developments needed by humanity and revealed by God. Therefore each must be considered as an authentic belief for us sent by God. Being one of the people selected by God to bring these 21 Revelations forward to the Christian, Islamic (and possibly Judaism and Hinduism) religious leaders and followers is an incredible honour and one which I genuinely appreciate. For this, I give thanks to God! There is little doubt in my mind that there are most likely other people also receiving these Revelations from God throughout the world at this stage and deciding what to do next. Please pray for them and for the support we all need.

Key New Revelations from God

It is appropriate, and I would claim necessary, for people to accept new genuine Revelations and inspired messages from God. We can't be scared to do so! If GOD is always seen as Number ONE above all of creation in all ways except sin; being absolutely holy, spiritual, and ethical, then we are doing the correct action by advising humanity of God's latest teachings. This isn't arguing in any way whatsoever to delete any previous religious teachings if these are still appropriate. It is what those religious leaders, scholars, and theologians, etc. find in their research, prayer, discernment, etc. into the newly offered 21 Revelations and some Inspired Messages. It is to add these to the list of religions' teachings already being taught and lived. God would have revealed these to his prophets and other holy, good people for dissemination to all people. For many readers, these four unique new teachings for Today will possibly, and maybe even considerably, challenge their faith and beliefs. This should be seen as a good thing! Please answer the challenge in the best non-violent way for you. (See the four referred to Revelations in four pages ahead, p.46ff.)

These updated teachings are added to God's Revelations already shared with us throughout the millennia. These now exist because the world has developed so significantly since the days of Jesus and Mahomad on our Earth. We need to celebrate the sharing of these teachings from God with us all. There must be no fear of God, or denial of God's latest messages, that these Revelations have been told to us Today. There may be challenges considered by the reader, and this is good. For many people, it is a part of their processes of developing an adult belief and faith.

God has asked me to invite all people, no matter their religion or denomination of an authentic religion or no religion at all, to accept these new Revelations as the Truth. All people, no matter their religion or no religion, are invited by God to become a part of this Revelatory occasion and exploration into the latest Truths sent from God.

Some of these latest Revelations have been espoused over the centuries in some form or another to various people, cultures, and religions worldwide. Book 1 introduces, and Book 3 details, the first listed 12 Revelations to me from God in 2016. The numbering and content of these Revelations will have a minimal but necessary change in this newest Book, i.e., Revelation #6 was not released until now, as per God's timeline. It has been added to the twenty-one Revelations at its normal #6 position.

Then we have the four latest revealed Revelations not having been seen by most followers of God, including me, before I received God's Revelations (and possibly others, yet unknown to me). From the Revelations, I have received, discernment, prayer, experiences and research. These seem to be both new or repeated from history and originals for Today. Some seem simple and are so, so essential for us now. Revelation #6 may also help with understanding those aspects of Mahomad's life we would consider as violence? Hopefully, this challenge will be entirely accepted by the experts as they analyse and eventually publish the new belief. When we include the other six received by the author in 2018 (See p208ff), there are 21 Revelations all together over those couple of years. God has asked through at least this author (and as previously noted, most likely through other people worldwide as well) that the leaders, theologians and scriptural scholars, etc., of both Christianity and Islam. This is also along with any other genuine religions, to advise the populations and religious faiths what the implications may be for the One and Only True God of all cultures and all followers of the **most challenging Revelations received – (see box on p.44).**

Along with readers and religious leaders. Just as people and cultures, etc. change over the centuries and millennia, religions also must develop and adapt to suit the world in which these religions are followed and celebrated, etc. Through developments which won't lose each religions' underlying theologies or faith stances – unless told otherwise by God or God's prophets and other holy people through Revelations and Inspired Messages. Their practices, liturgies and beliefs develop according to significant world changes, community lifestyles and true callings of their followers and other believers.

Yet the essential basics for all religions, which initially came directly from God historically and often lasted for millennia, must always maintain the position as critical teachings from God, (unless told otherwise by God). God's Revelations today will help various religions appreciate some newer 'up-to-date ones', as well as being relevant today and a key to our Love of God and all others. There are a number of these 21 Revelations which many people would not rightly consider to be new or exceptional in any everyday vital religious teachings from God, which God wanted to be highlighted for Today. These are therefore present to enhance, combine and remind us all of some of the wonder and majesty of the one and only GOD!!!

1. Incarnation Revelations of #15 - 'Jesus and Mahomad are GOD' (See p53ff, 90ff, 162ff, 181ff)

2. Revelation #6 - This Revelation will challenge many people as to their commitment to God and God's communities in particular. 'Die for what is right'. (See p233ff).

3. The author as a Prophet Statement (See p29ff, 103ff, 140ff)

4. God's photographic sun and cloud signs help inspire us to believe in God and His loving ways for each of us. God is challenging us to accept the Revelations and inspired messages from 'Him' through his prophets and good, holy people. Often, from the ordinary, come the extraordinary, Godly Revelations and challenges. (See PhotoBook 4 and GodTodaySeries.com website.)

21 Revelations from God - 2016 and 2018

God gave the author a total of 21 Revelations on two separate occasions over two and a half years, i.e. May 2016 (15 Revelations) and November 2018 (6 Revelations). God revealed the final six Revelations after Books One to Four were already published and available to the readers. None of this could have been anticipated, but it is God's way of lifting humanity to a higher level of existence and being placed in a position to make some incredible beliefs and doctrines become fundamental doctrine for the two largest religions worldwide, at least.

The remaining Revelations to the author in 2016 and 2018 will be introduced and explained in this Book. The explanations of these Revelations have been discerned over many decades, as well as through Truth bearing methods defined in this Book, and also used in the *Series'* previous books. Book 1 and Book 3 of this *'GOD Today' Series*, help explain 12 key Revelations plus other teachings from God, and the discernment processes involved.

God's Sun Signs Attract Us

Book 4, 'Where's God? Revelations Today Photobook Companion: GOD'S Signs', introduces spectacular God-given images probably not seen before by most people. I hadn't seen anything similar to these myself either. These are mostly raw, untouched images. The images came from two cameras – one android phone, the other an easily pocketed Panasonic Lumix. (Not an advertisement!) It is highly recommended to have Book 4 handy when reading Books 3 and 5. Or at least having read/viewed Book 4 prior to the other Series books.

The sun produced signs are brilliant!!! WOW, images!

My favourite book is, therefore, Book 4, which adds some unique and often challenging but accurate, spectacular, photographic images from God. This Book 4 should be seen concurrently with Books 1, 3 and now Book 5, if at all possible. *This very inspirational Book*

4 includes some of God's ways of highlighting and inspiring the author and the readers to explore and believe in the new Revelations.

In fact, in Book 4, readers should find uniquely soothing yet positively challenging and surprisingly unique images from God (with one exception - see below).

These could have occurred due to the sun's reflective and refracted light onto or within the cameras' lenses. Or even quite possibly directly as God's creation. Why? Simply because God can do anything! (Examples of these images may also be found on the *'God Today' Series* website and *God Today* Facebook page.)

Finding the Truth

These images highlight aspects which should encourage the reader to explore much further God's particular messages for Today. Some may seem more abstract, yet still, be incredibly authentic when observed with the others. These also may challenge the beliefs of many readers considerably. God desires that people accept these and support their various religious leaders, theologians, other key people charged with receiving and explaining God's latest Revelations within each religion and denomination of those religions and their followers.

The faithful, especially those from Christianity and Islam, need to find the Truth of these Revelations for their followers and other community members. *The critical focus of Revelation #15 is for Islam and Christianity. Yet it could also apply to other religions* showing particular interest in the Incarnation of God. (I would imagine this to be something quite exhilarating and possibly as real for many of these followers of different religions compared to Islam and Christianity.) And definitely so, when various other religions start to accept the modern-day 21 Revelations.

Book 5 also brings together the key points and teachings given by God to the author and developed in this *Series,* as clear and concise Revelations and inspired messages from God. God's aim is believed to purposely present some simple or exceptional teachings in easily understood ways, as introduced in Book 1. Being neither longwinded or too brief, but in a clear, non-complicated format, which presents God's latest Revelations honestly and clearly to Today's people.

Essential Appendices

There are eleven essential appendices in this latest Book; some edited from other books in the *'GOD Today' Series.* The main purpose of these is to help the reader who is keenly interested in more of the information provided in this *Series* and needs an easily readable refresher before Book 5. Or who hasn't yet been able to read the earlier books to allow this next Book 5 to stand alone? Or who may need a higher degree of background, all depending on the reader's choice? It is to help depth and appreciate the whereabouts of this Book's themes, which are set in Today's world and the divine world beyond our everyday lives. It details various necessary experiences of the author for setting this Book within the scope of the *'God Today' Series*. It also places the Book in the context of the whole *Series* by listing the various 'Contents pages' of each prior publication, plus the next Book to be released in this *'GOD Today' Series*, Book 6. Included in this *Series* is the content's list for that upcoming textbook, Book 6, *Love is the Meaning of Life: GOD's Love*, out in 2020/1. Book 7, the last photobook in this *Series*, Book Six's companion photobook, will be released in approximate 2021/2.

Many of the inspired messages from God commenced being revealed for the author on his twenty-fifth birthday. Both this story (*25th Birthday*, see Appendix 5) and the other essential story of 2016 (Appendix 2) initiated the development and presentation of this *Series*. Both the gifting of the Revelations' stories from God to the author (Appendices 2 and 5) are shared here to help with a necessary background for people to gain a proper appreciation of these messages from God. Statements like this and others may sometimes be revealed directly to the reader him/herself. These two, prominent, true stories have also been placed in this latest Book 5 so that the reader will have access to these two

> The faithful, especially those from Christianity and Islam, need to find the Truth of these Revelations for their followers and other community members.
> The critical focus of Revelation #15 is mainly for Islam and Christianity.
> Yet it could also apply to other religions showing particular interest in the Incarnation of God, etc…
> …This Book 5 also brings together the key points and teachings given by God to the author and developed in this *Series,* as clear and concise Revelations and inspired messages from God.

critical narratives necessary for an appropriate appreciation of the Revelations gained.

'Tears from God'

Karen, my wife, has also had input into the final presentations, mainly from an editorial perspective but also as a recipient of the Tears from God. The Tears, which we experience, mostly come when God is uniquely present while the author is writing the books, discussing the books together, or for various themes and explanations contained within or about the books. Also, as God can do anything that is Godly/Good, the Tears may come when unexpected, etc. These are explained in this fifth Book, as well.

To ignore these Tears from God for any reason is to challenge God.

We must never put God to the test!

For those fortunate to have experienced these Tears know what these mean because this is part of the Revelation process – people receiving these messages or feelings, etc. from God, need to spread God's Word in whatever way the recipients can do in their circumstances.

'God Today' Series Books' Release Dates

Due to a timeline for release dates of each Book being discerned by the author as required from God, each Book is being published according to when God 'tells' me that it is time. Books 6 and 7 are listed for 2020/1/2. Book 5 is now listed for July 2020. This allows for the *Series* to be fully released between 2016-2021/2.

Two Incarnations of God – Jesus and Mahomad

This latest Book 5 is a unique narration of author articles necessary to bring the key questions and possible answers together in one place – for a significant Revelation from God for all humanity. It begins with an introduction, which includes essential themes to appreciate the claims made in this Book. Next comes the major claim about the TWO INCARNATIONS of GOD being explored. Following these challenging Revelations is a detailed breakdown of the last six Revelations given directly to the author by God but not yet detailed for the reader in any of this *Series'* publications. To conclude, it was necessary to renumber three of these Revelations, including Revelations #6, #13 and #14, and which have only just been published in this Book Five - is due to the challenges met by the author for the level of understanding and appreciation required. Finally, are the eleven necessary appendices to assist with the clarity to be seen throughout.

Readers who haven't explored the previous books in this *Series* will be well assisted by the appendices to put critical points into perspective and to open the essential understandings to appreciate many very challenging Revelations from God.

As we are all at a variety of places in our relationship with God, this Book doesn't assume anything about each reader's experiences and journey to God. That is, apart from the prominent personal explorations people may be making through reading copies of this Book's *Series* and other similar themed books available Today.

Stand Alone Book 5

This latest Book 5 is a virtually stand-alone edition.

That is, it covers a number of the essential topics needed and which have been referred to a degree previously in earlier books within the Series, so that the reader may come to their, hopefully, enlightened position. This Book's appendices have been edited when needed from previous publications in this Series, for this Book's specific themes and detail required. Essential inclusions and adjustments for clarity within the Series have been made.

Nothing is forced! God never forces anyone to do anything. It is always up to the individual affected, as to their response from the offers given by God or others – with or without God's assistance. God gifts us the freedom to choose good and right over bad and wrong! It is our choices which so often cause the most incredible pain, anxiety and anguish to ourselves or others, through our wrong, accidentally or on purpose decisions.

The closer we get to God, the better and more appropriate are our decisions. Good begins to 'win over' evil more often.

The two central claims made in this Book will be considered quite revolutionary by many people – being both very personally and religiously challenging! But hopefully being seen as very genuinely authentic and real. The reader needs to appreciate the honesty with which these are shared. These are the Truth as given by God to the author.

The world is being challenged by God to change appropriately and to include these two Revelations legitimately.

Hence, Book 5 can be both a stand-alone text or an integral part of the whole *Series*. Does this often depend on how the reader has decided to follow this as a *Series* or just this one Book? The Series includes much more detail and explanation, whereas Book 5 contains enough detail to gain a general appreciation of the Series' critical points.

No Illegitimate Violence Allowed by God

The biggest mistake people can make these days is to react excessively and even possibly violently as a result of the teachings and nature of the two significant Revelations from God for Today.

All people are reminded that violence is not an option from God. God is the one and only judge and 'prosecutor' for each person at the time of their death. Yet people's lifestyles are also considered. What we have said and done etc. are also essential to God's decision. Those who love God and creation and are close to God will be rewarded through God's loving assistance and guidance on their life's pathways, eventually leading to Heaven. Forgiveness requested from God is essential for us to show our genuine Love for God legitimately.

Pray in peace with God for an appropriate appreciation of these new Revelations and how each will enhance and bring people and religions much closer together.

To verbally or physically attack anyone over a religious issue, belief or practice etc. is EVIL!!! The ABSOLUTELY LOVING GOD needs us ALL to act out of LOVE - not EVIL – NO VIOLENCE.

On a rare occasion, there may be a need for significant non-violent reaction to people who have violently blasphemed against God or threatened others with violence. Only on very limited circumstances is defensive power permitted, e.g. self-defence - in any of our genuine religions and for a legitimate reason. God emphasises LOVE as the answer to everything – i.e. out of the LOVE of God…

Something remarkable happens. What God does and requires from us begins to become more apparent, until the person accepts God's challenge. This is essential. God is always calling us peacefully. Trust God and follow God's way. Ask God for as much assistance as you possibly need. Then allow God to assist in any way God chooses. At times, it is not what we imagined.

Violence often occurs when people are ignorant of the Truth or have no real intention of following their historical religion's developing beliefs, new or otherwise, given by God Today. Some people are way too easily convinced to do evil. This often occurs resulting from poor religious, family or communal leadership, inferior examples given by the followers of God, greed, not caring for the afterlife and hence not accepting God's call etc. God requires us to be exceptional humans sharing this most incredible planet for our physical lives – before sharing the awesome divine experience with God after death – forever!!!.

Faithful Challenged

Too many of the faithful will have genuine trouble accepting these two new Revelations, yet this acceptance is precisely what God commands.

It appears to have been quite a long time since God has revealed anything of major significance to the various religions, based on the lack of any evidence we should have of any such happenings. However, this may not be so either. We should maintain our scope of wonder for and with God to be aware of such possible major significance occurring or having occurred. It, therefore, makes sense, timewise, that the world now needs various updates/developments from God. Our society has changed these past centuries massively. The world and its beliefs and challenges have changed considerably since the original Revelations and inspired messages were revealed from God millennia ago. God has shared these latest Revelations with all of us. Yet, the basics haven't changed much over time.

'GOD Today' Series

A series of eight books, including five nonfiction and three photobooks, plus a video series by Bryan Foster, released between 2016 and 2021/2.

OUT NOW

1God.world: One God for All (2016)

Mt Warning God's Revelation: Photobook Companion to '1God.world' (2017)

Where's GOD? Revelations Today (2018)

Where's GOD? Revelations Today Photobook Companion: GOD Signs (1 & 2 eds) (2018)

'GOD Today' Video Series (2018)

Jesus and Mahomad are GOD (2020)

OUT 2020-2022

Love is The Meaning of Life: GOD'S Love (2nd ed) (2020)

Love is The Meaning of Life GOD's Love: Photobook Companion (2020/1)

Wisdom made real: A Lifetime of Godly Hints and Tips for Us All (Working Title) (2021/2)

Love is The Meaning of Life (1st ed) (late 2020/early 2021)

(An edited and shortened version – includes an introduction to God's Love for the non-believer and those with doubts. The Book is an edited version of the 2nd ed.)

"GOD Today" Series' Overviews

1God.world: One God for All introduced in detail the most important of the Revelations from God for Today and challenged the reader to search and find God through other people, nature and God's inspired messages. It introduced the author and shared twenty-six of his personal, spiritual, finding-God stories. A series of inspired messages discerned by the author over his lifetime was shared. (See Appendix 4 for Contents.)

Mt Warning God's Revelation: Photobook Companion to '1God.world' is a photographic exploration around Mt Warning taken over three years, culminating in the Revelations from God on the plains at the foot of the mountain one cold night in May, 2016. It is a photographic and written story of the spectacular and spiritually inspiring Mt Warning and its surrounding towns, landscapes and fauna. Images are taken from all angles around its 72km base and road up to the walking track.

Where's GOD? Revelations Today invites the reader to continue the journey of exploring who and where God is for them and what are God's messages for Today's world. It details twelve Revelations from God for Today introduced in the previous two books. A collection of another six inspired messages received within that same 24-hour revelation period is shared. A key focus is on assisting the reader in their appreciation, understanding and searches for God in Today's world. (See Appendix 7 for Contents)

Where's GOD? Revelations Today Photobook Companion: GOD Signs, surprises the reader with exceptional and unique photographic images, formed by God and possibly from various reflections and refractions of the sun in this popular 50-page coloured photobook. Some sun-arrows formed across the author, along with spectacular sun shapes created in the sky. These occurred at three venues on the plains and at the foot of Mt Warning, Cabarita and Kingscliff beaches, as well as on Straddie, at Cylinder Beach, North Stradbroke Island and inland at Texas on the Queensland/New South Wales border.

The sun is seen as central for many people in their imagining and discerning of God and God's beyond-our-reality's awesome powers. Other spectacular sunrise and sunset images are shared from Australia and Canada. This is a must-read book, which supports and highlights many aspects in each Book in this 'GOD Today' *Series*. (See Appendix 8 for Contents)

Jesus and Mahomad are GOD A massive challenge for over fifty per cent of the world's population covering Christianity and Islam alike is now issued in *the most important Book of this Series*. The present-day prophet and God's Incarnations will surprise many readers. The solution sort is also mind-enhancing. The remaining Revelations of the twenty-one Revelations complete those discussed in the previous Books, One and Three. Prayer and our relationship with God and the Incarnate God (Jesus and Mahomad) hold critical possibilities for our future world. The world's religious leaders and scholars will need to redefine, after discerning, some essential beliefs and practices now and followed up quickly with the education of the populations.

Love is The Meaning of Life: GOD'S Love (2nd ed) is planned for release around December 2020. A significant exploration of what Love is and how it often affects us all introduces this Book. There is a major discussion on the types of Love, its positive and sometimes negative impacts, and how we can grow in true Love throughout our lifetimes with our special loved ones, family, friends, colleagues, communities and of course God. God is seen as the absolute lover who loves us all equally and desires, ideally our perfect union on this Earth and ultimately with God in Heaven. God's Love and relationship with humanity are explored in detail. It is God's Love shared with us all, which help all of us develop a real closeness with God, our loved ones, friends and colleagues. (See Appendix 9 for Contents)

***Love is The Meaning of Life GOD'S Love: Photobook Companion* (Working Title) (2020/1)** is still in the early planning stages. It will strongly support the textbook through significant photographic images. The release date is planned for late 2020/early 2021. The images will sometimes be quite challenging. Combined with various literary genres used to enhance the photos, this Book will be strong support for those wishing for more real, genuine Love in their lives and the world as a whole. Emphasis is on how God, being Absolute Love, can help us in all our relationships with each other and with God.

Wisdom Made Real: A Lifetime of Godly Hints and Tips for Us All (Working Title) (2021-2)

The final Book 8 explores various statements of Wisdom associated with God, Love, Life and Eternity. It shows how Wisdom can vary over a person's lifetime. For a start, Book 8 will assist with enabling the reader to explore and discern incredibly important philosophical and everyday lifestyle statements, feelings, emotions, commitments, ethics and values.

Love is from GOD. GOD is ABSOLUTE LOVE! Everything real and genuine we know about Love and its impact on us comes from knowing God. Every experience we have of Love is from God – is of God with us.

Love is The Meaning of Life (1st ed) (2020/1)

This primarily secular based edition is not an actual part of the Series, yet is needed to assist readers who may find God a real challenge. They may not believe in God, or they may have significant issues with God. God is mentioned, hopefully not in a too challenging way, but in such a way as to inspire further exploration about God's place in Love, life, and death. But enough for the reader to maybe want to explore these concepts themselves further. The text is virtually the same as the Book's 2nd edition, but with less of the considerable God themes. Written to detail the Love theme in everyday life and to maybe even challenge the reader to explore the God option in more depth when ready once gently challenged. Reader to explore the God option in more depth when ready once gently challenged.

Prayer and our relationships with the Incarnate God -

Jesus and Mahomad -

Hold key essential possibilities for the future of this world

And its people.

Seek from God a personal, informed understanding…

We must ACT NOW!!!

Introduction

What will you find new and challenging in this latest Book 5? Let's begin with Revelation # 15's topic from May, 2016 – *Jesus and Mahomad are God?* This is an incredible new Revelation from God and probably unheard of as a possibility by most of the world's religious faithful. The readers will be encouraged to go as deeply as they are interested in these topics. Exploring and supporting God's Incarnation as Jesus and Mahomad.

The Primary source of most of the included information in this Book Five, along with the rest of this *Series*, is GOD! Other information gathered from different sources is listed along with God in the Bibliography.

The author aims to assist people throughout this Book Five, no matter wherever they are on the 'understanding God continuum', to reach higher into the God/Divine realm.

Reaching towards and becoming one with God through our prayer, beliefs, actions, and lifestyle, adds so much depth to a person's life, relationships, and accepting God's equal Love for everyone, everywhere. It starts with the belief in God as the absolute power within and beyond creation! God always was! God is now! God is forever 'everywhere'!

All that is written in this Book Five, from the *'GOD Today' Series* of eight books and photobooks, *have come directly from God if a Revelation*. Or, if these are *discerned from God* by the author, each is then *an inspired message from God,* i.e., *God working spiritually within your true self and your soul.*

Critical topics covered throughout this publication include:

- The Truth from God, as received by the author.
- Jesus and Mahomad are Incarnations of God, i.e., they are God become human for a specific, limited time in history.
- The author is seriously considering an incredibly humbling prophetic request

from God - this now gives added strength and wisdom for these proclamations.

- 21 Revelations directly from God and received over two years, 2016 (15) and 2018 (6) – there are considered explanations for those not yet detailed in earlier books.
- Religious leaders, scholars, theologians, etc. from at least Christianity and Islam, but also other interested religions and even non-religious secularists, need to delve deeply into Revelation #15 mainly, due to its controversial nature and its significance to God. *My role is to promulgate the Revelations received, in particular #15, to these people, along with others interested from all walks of life.*
- There is even a possibility that this process working closely together could bring all the involved religions to become more unified and less separated from each other. These religions could start the process of working closely together in a very divided world, which is only getting worse.

Due to the complexities and precise direction given by God, the 21 Revelations revealed to the author are being released as an all-encompassing series, *'GOD Today' Series* (for the years from 2016 to 2021/2). This, Book Five in the *Series*, allows for a stand-alone approach. Key concepts and the necessary detail of the topics see various *'GOD Today' Series'* quotes/author's articles noted. This allows for an overview of the vital background explanations included in this Book. The *Jesus and Mahomad are God* publication has enough general and specific detail for the reader to gain a good understanding of the nine new Revelations in this Book. Details of the previous 12 Revelations were explained in Book Three.

It would be beneficial for readers of this *'GOD Today' Series,* to have Photobook Four - *Where's God? Revelations Today Photobook Companion: GOD Signs* (2018), to view incredibly unique images, some almost unbelievable. There is a major collection of unique and spectacular sun and cloud combined images sent by God to the author through the photographic images taken.

Most pictures are believed to be unseen by a majority of people at this stage! These were undoubtedly new, exciting but challenging also, to both Karen, my wife, and me. These surprising details were not seen while photographing but were seen on our laptops at the day's end. Incidentally, two cameras were used, an android mobile phone/cell phone and a Panasonic Lumix.

These images go some way to encouraging and inspiring the reader to explore this GOD Series. Many of the photos seem to be quite unreal and not possible, or just too coincidental but yet still impressive and come from God. Very inspirational and supporting of God's invitation to believe the images and the Revelations shared.

Many people won't believe these images are possible. Definitely worth the viewing, though. It is anticipated that these will both challenge you and excite you. You'll most likely be inspired and probably note at some level the commonly used, 'OMG/Oh My God!' This reaction would be quite different to when this abbreviation or phrase is usually used for anything exceptionally surprising or challenging, in the secular world these days, etc. In the latest photobook (Book 4), it would most likely be a correct response to something quite spectacular, enjoyable, and informative in a religious response from God. (See Appendix 11)

(Also see GodTodaySeries.com website for an introduction to some of these images in colour. Book 4 is an all-colour photobook production. A JesusAndMahomadAreGOD.com website will have been developed closer to the publication of this Book 5.)

'Where's God? Revelations Today Photobook Companion: GOD Signs' (2018) includes sun arrows, rays, flares, Easter sky crosses, and double rainbows. All are sending various messages to the reader. These are quite different from what you might expect, with a number very inspiring. Reading the earlier books will help to gain a deeper appreciation of the developing topics, and how these may affect you, I imagine you as the positive 'God Lover/Searcher'. There are also some quotes from previous Books to assist the reader with

essential background information to appreciate this latest Book 5.

There is a significant need to bring God back to the front and centre of societal leadership needs. The secular society is making many uninformed, and non-divinely influenced decisions, which have major impacts on the population, often of a negative outcome. What do we need from God? How can we gain this? What does each person need to do? Etc.

In the *'GOD Today' Series'* first four books, twelve out of fifteen initial Revelations received by the author in 2016 have been emphasised. The next upcoming two books, Books 6 and 7, include a photobook in this *Series* which goes to the core of Love, and God's loving place in our world. It highlights what Love and forgiveness and loving relationships in particular are and how Love has an impact on every individual and community. The key theme is that *Love is the Meaning of Life: [i.e.] GOD'S Love (2020).*

The final Book 8 explores various statements of Wisdom associated with God, Love, Life and

Eternity. It shows how Wisdom can vary over a person's lifetime. For a start, Book 8 will assist with enabling the reader to explore and discern incredibly important philosophical and everyday lifestyle statements, feelings, emotions, commitments, ethics and values.

Love is from GOD. GOD is ABSOLUTE LOVE! Everything real and genuine we know about Love and its impact on us comes from God. Every experience we have of Love is from God – is of God with us.

This current Book Five highlights some very essential common beliefs as well as new beliefs, which have not been considered in any real depth beforehand by religious leaders and scholars, (as far as the author is aware).

For many people, these will be too contentious and may even tear at their inner beliefs. However, because all these Revelations have come directly from our Loving God, each must be considered very important to God and hence for us also. These Revelations from God are so significant for our modern world that these have inspired a series of books and videos as explanations to share worldwide.

It is necessary and essential for our world to move forward in peace and enlightenment to appreciate and act upon these four very significant new Revelations from God. (See also Appendices 1, 2, and 5, includes the 2016 Revelations' experience.)

The critical belief, which will challenge many people, is based on the link between Jesus, Mahomad*, and God.

(*Reminder: The spelling variation of 'Mahomad*' was how it was passed from God as I transcribed its receival with the 15 Revelations in May 2016.)

No longer can Christianity claim to have God becoming incarnate only in Jesus Christ. From the latest Revelations from God, Islam's Mahomad is God, and Jesus the Christ is God too. Twice in history. We are now told by God in these Revelations, that God has become

Incarnate, once as Jesus around 3BCE and the next time around 570CE as Mahomad. (See Revelation #15, p90ff, 181ff)

I received this Revelation #15 directly from God in the early morning of the 29 May, 2016. (Appendix 2, p.272ff) Another six inspired messages were also received prior to that night, in the afternoon of 28 May, (Appendix 3, p.277ff) before the fifteen Revelations being received the next early morning. Six more arrived in November, 2018.

God has made it clear to me that my role is to promulgate these 21 Revelations, variously inspired messages, and explanations to Today's world. Tears from God (See p.52ff, 124ff) on numerous occasions over the past five years, in particular, along with other evidence of proof, particularly the sun and cloud inspirational signs, were the main proof offered from God for the authenticity of the Revelations. (See p36ff, p. 46-7, p.110ff - 'Are the Revelations and inspired messages contained in this Series the Truth from God? - Genuine and authentic explanations').

It is then up to the various religions' scholars, leaders, faithful, etc. to develop the theology resulting from these Revelations and inspired messages. The two critical religions impacted by these promulgations from God are Christianity and Islam. There is also a special place for both Judaism and Hinduism to be invited to the table. Both believe in One God only. Hinduism's Brahman is God manifested in all its other lower gods, yet Brahman is still the One God. Judaism's One God is Yahweh.

God, Allah, Yahweh, and Brahman are all the same One and Only God. Each is a different religion's name for the Only God ever and forever for all faiths and all cultures.

God is the Only God of all religions. One God for All!!!

It is now time to promulgate this latest extraordinary Revelation #15. Leaders, scholars, and holy people, etc. in both Islam and Christianity need to meet together, pray, meditate, research, discuss, theologise, discern and eventually promulgate this most loving of all commandments from God. To then clearly explain and teach this particular belief as to the

Truth. It came directly from God to the author. God doesn't only speak to religious academics and leaders. People of varying religious backgrounds and interests are also spoken to by God. This author, respectively being one on these occasions.

God has instructed that the world is ready and needs to accept this crucial divine belief. (See p.110ff for accuracy of the Truth of these Revelations.)

God's passing these Revelations on to the author, shows that the world is ready for this Revelation from God. It makes so much sense to accept, without questioning God, that this is true. Once we honestly believe that a Revelation is the Truth from God and an informed conscience or deep spiritual belief supports this fully, we have no right to question or challenge God in any way what-so-ever. We cannot put God to the test! We can ask for assistance to understand and appreciate it, though.

The author of this Book 5 was also challenged to accept and then promulgate these new teachings — this new theology for both Christianity and

Islam. And hence for the world in general. It is very challenging for any human to put this out there to the world for fear of ridicule, bullying, and other negatively reactionary responses. Yet, it is the latest Truth from God to be promulgated and hence will be done.

Just as for the author, and the reader may initially have difficulties accepting it entirely for a while. Ask God for assistance, if needed. I now believe it thoroughly and am excited about how this needs to bring at least the two largest religions in the world together in a rather significant way due to the quality of Revelation #15. Hopefully, the other significant faiths will see the Light and join in with Islam and Christianity on their quest for the Incarnate God initially, followed by many of the other Revelations and inspired messages included in this text.

The religious leaders and scholars of any religion accepting of this Truth, are required to state the new belief as told directly to me by God and to then stand by it to highlight its Truth. Each Revelation is directly from God, as indicated. It is now up to the vital leadership, scriptural scholars and theologians, etc. within both Islam and Christianity (and other religions if desired by these other faiths) to analyse what is in the 21 Revelations, particularly #15. In contrast, the Revelations' explanations are based on the author's discerned beliefs, acquired over decades, and based on so many experiences with God, mostly through prayer, life experiences, academia, Revelations, and inspired messages.

Both Christian and Muslim leaders, theologians, and scriptural scholars need to explain how it is possible and how it is the Truth. This will bring the two largest world religions together in unique ways, as has never occurred with them before on this anticipated level.

There is an invitation for any other genuine religion to come to the table, too, particularly Hindus and Jews who both believe in One God also.

As the world comes closer together and there develops the essential belief of One God for all religions, times and beliefs, this new foundational faith of God Incarnate in Islam and Christianity needs to be espoused and be seen as essential for humankind – and acted on!

God needed this to be withheld for centuries until the right time arrived. Through this Revelation, it has shown now to be that time.

The world has been previously incapable of handling this Revelation without the prospect of significant conflict and destruction.

'Jesus and Mahomad are GOD' – and are totally and equally ONE. Each is absolutely the ONE SAME GOD. Jesus and Mahomad are God Incarnate, i.e., God became human for two highly significant periods in history – as Jesus and Mahomad – that we know of so far, i.e., as the situation appears to us now. There certainly could be other Incarnations of God throughout the world now and in the past, or as yet to come in the future!

(Also see Appendix 4 - Author's Life Events Leading to 'GOD Today' Series.) (A short autobiography.)

Suggested Sections and Articles for the Reader – depending on the books read in this *Series*:

1. Those who have read the first four books would best read: Jesus and Mahomad are GOD; 21 Revelations for Today Overview for the background; Introduction; and your selection of pages in the Appendices.
2. Those who are new to the Series, it is best to read everything in the *Series* to gain the ultimate experience offered from God. However, your order of sections to read could change depending on your interests. *Book Five does stand alone in the Series if desired. Book Four has essential and striking images from God* – including the sun and cloud images with arrows, flares, rainbows and rays – many physically through or across the author.
3. Those who have read only one Book in this *Series* – are recommended to read all of

Book Five except those included sections you have seen before. Obtaining Book 4 would help deepen your experience overall, significantly.

Referencing Note

The reader will notice a general minimalisation of academic references. Where helpful, these are included. However, most of the content in this Book is either directly from God as Revelations or Inspired Messages discerned by the author, making considerable use of the

primary source of all primary sources available - GOD.

There are referrals back to Books 1 to 4 and various appendices from the *'GOD Today' Series*, as a necessity of background knowledge needed to hopefully assist the reader to understand and appreciate what God has done for today's people worldwide. These incorporate all genuine religions, in whatever depth they decide to be involved.

God is telling the world that the right time for God's influence on humanity is now!!!

It is GOD'S Time.

NOW!

God requests us to

Reflect on Revelation #15 specifically

along with the

21 Revelations

(Introduced below…)

Revelation #15

Revelation #15 from God to the author in May 2016

Jesus is God [*]

Brahma[/n] is God

Yahweh is God

Mahomad/Allah is God [*]

Mahomad is Allah is God.

Jesus and Mahamod is God.

[*] Don't doubt this

(*) Asterix stands for the joining of these two Revelations (with lines on the originally written Revelations) i.e. to join lines beginning with 'Jesus' and 'Mahomad'. Plus the instruction to not doubt these two lines' authenticity.

Spelling and punctuation are exactly as written from the Revelation.

Jesus is GOD!
Mahomad is GOD!

There is only 1 God for:
* all religions
* all people
* all cultures
* all time

FOREVER!!!

Both Christian and Muslim religious leaders, theologians and scriptural scholars etc. need to explain what Revelation #15 means for today's world, how it is possible and how it is the Truth from God…

There must also be room for other genuine religions to come to the table too,

particularly Hindus and Jews who also both believe in One God –
as a starting point.

These two incredible Incarnate GOD Revelations where God becomes fully human are explained.

The Truth of these as part of the 21 Revelations received in May 2016, and November 2018 will be clarified.

The author's role in the receival of these 21 Revelations and the dissemination will be explained.

Why and how is the author a part of this promulgation?

How can everyone gain as a result of these?

Bryan Foster

GOD

GIFTS

US

LOVE

Love
Faith
Hope
Peace
Forgiveness
Truth
Empathy
Compassion
...

Islam's Mahomad is God,

Christianity's Jesus Christ is God.

…God became Incarnate,

once as Jesus around 3BCE

and the next time as Mahomad around 570CE.

Author and Truths

Author

Bryan Foster and I have been married for forty-two years. We have three adult children and six grandchildren. Our two eldest adult children are teachers, while our third is studying science at university.

Bryan concentrates on his writings now, having permanently retired from the teaching of religion after 42 years. His main Series now is the *'GOD Today' Series* of seven to eight books/photobooks which began being compiled in 2016 and will conclude in 2021/2. The writings include nonfiction books, photobooks, videos, websites and social networking platforms. *Jesus and Mahomad are GOD* is the fifth Book in the *Series*.

Bryan has played a significant role in religious schools, parishes and the deanery. He taught religion for forty-two years, including thirty years of 'Study of Religion' to years/grades 11-12, been a primary/elementary school principal twice and an assistant principal for religious education in secondary/high school. Bryan has been a president and secretary of both parishes and deanery pastoral councils, as well as president of his children's primary school's Parents and Friends Association, twice.

On the early morning of the 29 May 2016, Bryan received 15 Revelations from God. Each was written down as he was told to do by God. A 'bombshell' of a statement was also written halfway through receiving the Revelations. It was out of the blue but incredibly powerful. It wasn't until last year, 2019, that Bryan has come to accept its content, which seems to go against all those inherent appreciations of present-day beliefs of individuals and communities.

It stated that "I am a prophet prophets are true." This statement has remained there in his Revelation notes from God for almost four years without him realising the implications and reality of it.

After much reflection and discernment of what is the Truth, it now places much onus on Bryan to fully accept it and do what is required to promulgate these Revelations to the world. It all came together for him on Easter Sunday Eve in 2019 at his home on the Gold Coast, Australia. Tears from God (p.52ff, p.124ff) clinched the acceptance of this Revelation for both Bryan and me. Bryan accepted this position and is very humbled and excited by it. He now needs to promulgate these messages for God. This promulgation particularly needs to highlight the (until now) unpublished Revelation #15 (See p.90ff, p181ff – this book's theme.) It was the last Revelation received in May, 2016.

For accuracy, the spelling and punctuation are precisely as revealed in the Revelations from God. (N.B. The exact words, spelling and grammar from God are given here as Revelations. Why the variation in minor spelling from the norm? We don't know.)

Bryan received another six Revelations from God two and a half years later on 3 November 2018. These concentrate on God and our relationship with God.

In general terms, the first 14 Revelations are to do with people, their respect and honesty for God and each other, how people behave and God's messages for a world in need. The next seven are primarily based on God as the ABSOLUTE ALMIGHTY GOD with authority beyond any imagining by us and our response to God – ABSOLUTE LOVE, OBEDIENCE, BELIEF, SUBMISSION and FORGIVENESS of self and others.

The next few articles in this Book, along with the appendices, are essential for the reader to obtain the necessary background knowledge and appreciation of specific topics needed to appreciate all 21 Revelations revealed to the author. The credibility of each is assured through God's sent Tears from God and other forms of 'proof', which are explained in this Book. (See p.36ff, p.46ff, p.110ff, p.265ff)

Also, Bryan's discerned understanding of each, and the impact these following articles have on him, and on his anticipated readers are significant. There are three essential edited extracts from the author's previous books in this

'GOD Today' Series. Those who have been following the *Series* will probably only need to scan over these to update the necessary concepts and content revealed from God at this discovery stage.

These details and revealed Truths from God set the scene for the Two Incarnations of God one for Christians and the other for Muslims, primarily that Jesus and Mahomad are both God and from God. These Truths are also for any genuine religion and anyone else authentically interested, so they can benefit from this Revelation.

Author's Academic Qualifications:

Master of Education (Religious Education)
Bachelor of Education
Graduate Diploma of Religious Education
Diploma of Religious Education
Diploma of Teaching

(by Karen Foster, Bryan's wife of 42 years)

Bryan Foster

"I am a prophet Prophets are true."

[Punctuation is as received from God.]

This statement has remained there on the first of two pages of the Revelations from God received in 2016

for almost four years until recently

without the author realising the implications and its possible realities.

The impact on me has been overwhelmingly palpable, beautiful and inspirational.

Time will tell how this will eventuate.

An incredible challenge for the author and those religious leaders who become involved in discerning and explaining the latest 21 Revelations.

Keep it Simple – KIS
(Keep it Simple - for God's sake.)

This world is way too good at complicating the whole message from God.

Many of humanity love to dissect everything said by God. Everything taught by God. Everything which is believed comes from God. Unfortunately, their accuracy is often misleading, wrong, or way too complicated for its audience of readers.

In every religion, the theological studies are an integral and most important aspect of that religion. But why does it have to get so complicated?

Yes, we all need help with explanations, mainly when the scriptural reference or theology is complicated or seems confused. Scriptural and theological experts are required to interpret and then explain the messages. These people should have the required scholarship, knowledge, and discernment to share these teachings in clear, easy to appreciate, language.

Excellent teachers, leaders, and theologians of all faiths must be able to explain the messages in simple, easy to understand and appreciate ways. Ways that help the individual and the community to believe and live the messages.

It seems that historically people appeared to be so afraid of God that they needed to overreach on the explanations of these beliefs, teachings, and experiences, etc. Through needing to be as correct as possible, they often complicated a simple message. They often believed that they were directly inspired by God to write what they were 'told'. On many occasions, this was no doubt correct, but there seem to be far too many words, and complicated explanations, for everything to be needed. Confusion sometimes abounds.

It seems to be that the unnecessary detail may even have been a justification for someone's career, place within society or position within a particular religion! Or maybe that the message has just become so complicated that we need to reinterpret or explain it!

Keep it simple!

Having stated this most essential of writing approaches used in this *'GOD Today' Series* as crucial, i.e., keep it simple, we now come to a point where this approach is needed more than ever before.

Knowing what the Revelation #15 is, and how much of a challenge it will be, particularly for the Christian and Islamic leaders and followers, we need to actively encourage those critical people charged with explaining and implementing this Revelation to be open, transparent and willing to keep the inspired Revelation simple and easy for all people to understand and support.

However, the simplicity of taking this to the people may need some detailed academic study, research, and writing before it is explained simply in their chosen formats.

Each religion which takes this essential, genuine belief on board and makes it one of their fundamental teachings will have the unconditional support of God. They need to keep God in the process and be open and willing to listen to God and others inspired by God, to fully tease out the implications and necessities of its implementation within religions and communities today.

There is considerable Wisdom about God and God's messages in each genuine religion and in each follower within that religion. Also, in the sacred writings of the faith and the teachings, practices and ritual of each religion.

As the world becomes more educated and individualistic, members, communities and societies within this world also become more critical of much that is institutional. This criticism is particularly of institutions with considerable history. Religion is one of, if not, the oldest of most cultures' institutions. It is often the first to be attacked from so many fronts.

What then are the messages from God for this modern world? Many of these were explored throughout Books 1 to 4 in this 'God Today' Series. Revelations #1 to #12 are highlighted in Book 3, *Where's God? Revelations Today (2018)*.

Revelations 13 to 21 are detailed in this latest Book, Book 5.

These are often seen as simple statements but usually not so easily accomplished in practice.

I have been convinced through my discernment and prayer life that this is what God wants for us – to Keep It Simple – KiS.

Hopefully, you will agree that this Book uses this method – neither too complicated nor too simple.

(Edited Extract from *Where's God? Revelations Today,* by Bryan Foster, 2018, p. 31-32.)

As the world becomes more educated and individualistic, people, communities and societies within this world also become more critical of much that is institutional.

This criticism is particularly of institutions with considerable history.

Religion is one of, if not, the oldest of most cultures' institutions. It is often the first to be attacked from so many fronts.

Are the Revelations and Inspired Messages contained in this Series the Truth from God?

Genuine and authentic explanations?

As an author, extolling the Revelations and inspired messages from God is a most challenging task. It goes well beyond my reflective writing of some thoughts and meanings. It goes to the whole core of appreciating ourselves, humanity and our association with God. To claim the authority to do so is a massive personal challenge. Rest assured it hasn't been done lightly. There is considerable truly heartfelt anxiety. *In my heart of hearts, my soul of soul, I genuinely believe in everything written in this publication wholeheartedly.*

The collection is one author's Revelations and inspired messages from God. Others throughout the world will also probably be receiving similar Revelations and inspired messages. Some may put these into publications. We all have our ways of dealing with and propagating what we receive.

All people can receive God's messages and Revelations. The big question for each person is, Am I ready and open to receiving messages or Revelations from God? Would I know when I received any? What would I do with these if and when I had similar experiences to this author? God inspires us in so many ways, mainly through other people and nature. Am I aware of inspired messages from God through others and our world?

These Revelations and inspired messages revealed to me have been developing over at least forty years. It is not something which has just ensued. The culmination so far has been the 21 Revelations from 2016 to 2018 at Murwillumbah Showgrounds and the Mt Warning Rainforest Park in NSW, Australia.

The key reasons for believing that these Revelations and inspired messages are from God is explained in more detail. The specific reasons below are followed by the detail of each subsequently.

- the 25th birthday experience and Revelation of God in May 1982 (Appendix 5);

- the Tears from God experiences, which have been growing in intensity and frequency, especially in the most recent years;
- the recent spectacular photographic images highlighting metaphorical or direct links with God;
- coincidences and signs from God over many years, especially in these past four years;
- the Revelations from God at the foot of Mt Warning in May 2016 and November 2018;
- the longevity without any personal doubt of my strong association with God;
- the personal career/vocation, 42 years teaching religion from years 1-12, including 30 years of Study of Religion to senior years 11-12;
- holding senior leadership positions in religious schools and parishes;
- prayer and meditation throughout and

- the continued strong support and agreement from my wife, Karen, and our families.

Each of these reasons supports the belief in either the Revelation or inspired messages being from God. God never forces anyone to believe anything. There is a level of 'proof' but also the mystery of the faith with any Revelation or inspired message from God. Therefore, it is through the combinations of these reasons and others, that God's unique presence is experienced with the outcomes of each needed to be shared. Having always been close to God, or at least in my teens on the fringes, allows for that openness to hear and know intrinsically when something is legitimately from God.

The 25th birthday experience is explained in detail in Appendix 5. The longevity of living without any doubt about God since that 25th birthday experience is quite significant, I believe. Since that 1982 experience, when God came to many students, staff and also me on the schools' Commitment Day' is an exceptional occasion.

The unique connection with God came about when prayed over by a charismatic religious sister/school principal who also had a masters degree in psychology. There has been absolutely no doubt about God's existence or God's absolute equal love for each human person throughout history. This 1982 revelatory moment was when I first truly experienced Tears from God in such depth. It also included the incredible warmth flowing from Sister's hands placed on the top of my head downwards through my whole body.

From that moment, over thirty-five years ago, there have been some tough and challenging times, as there are for everyone over their lifetimes. For me, these were mainly of personal health and financial types. Some were life-threatening or life-changing beyond any expectation or plan. There was also the average life challenging experiences of others. These range from family to the global. The global challenges needing to be worked-through include war, poverty and other injustices throughout the world and God's place with all these. Then there are the direct challenges personally in your beliefs, particularly from atheists. Members of this group are becoming particularly vicious and hate-filled towards anyone who espouses faith in God. You have to wonder why this is their form of defence/attack? There must be something more – do they feel guilty? Insecure? Ignorant? Unloved? Intellectually challenge? I just so wish they could be open and deliberately give God a go. I have to challenge these people, out of love for God and the Truth. Stop hiding from the Truth. The Truth will set you free!!! For me, this hateful reaction was experienced directly when I opened myself up to various religious sites on social media to introduce my first *GOD Today' Series* book, *1God.world: One God for All in 2016.*

The Tears from God experiences have been growing in intensity and regularity in recent years. These were initially experienced in 'introductory' levels from about the age of fifteen in year ten when I first wondered if I would like to join the priesthood, through to a higher level while at College in my late teenage years. One significant and influential event while at College was visiting a Sunday night charismatic mass where people were being healed through the Holy Spirit. The 25th birthday moment was the first significant Tears from God moment for me. Since then, similar sorts of occasions have been potent and enhancing. Each shows those extraordinary moments of pure bliss and the presence of God.

The Tears from God is the primary means of knowing of God's unique presence and occasion of confirming those Revelations or inspired messages.

In 2016 at the foot of Mt Warning, I was awoken and told by God in my mind's eye to write down precisely as God sent me the Revelations. The early morning encounter with God is explained in detail shortly in the 'Mt Warning…' story. (See Appendix 2.) This supernatural Revelation was confirmed the following morning at a First Communion Mass in the nearby church in which I married Karen forty-two years ago this year – through a Tears from God moment. Once again, two years later, more Revelations occurred at the foot of Mt Warning. These are those numbered sixteen to twenty-one. (See p.208ff)

There have been some different experiences, often recorded as photographs and featuring the sun, which seems to show God telling a story or offering a particular message. This message may be metaphorical or literal. Often it is God giving a sign of support, or confirmation of that specific message. A point of encouragement to the message's authenticity and the need for it to be shared with others. In my particular case, the need to accept my place in the scheme of God's plan and to go and do whatever is required to propagate the Revelation or message is also a genuine aspect!

In 2018 there were five quite similar sunlight events to each other, in close time proximity. One occurred at the foot of Mt Warning just after sunrise, another at Texas on the NSW/Queensland border, a third was at Straddie, North Stradbroke Island. In contrast, another two occurred at Kingscliff and Cabarita beaches in northern New South Wales, close to

Mt Warning, Australia. I believe that these images are part of the overall methods God uses to make particular points. These are just one method of many though.

Coincidences and signs often point to special moments. In *Where's God? Revelations Today Photobook Companion: GOD Signs (2nd ed)* these are explored along with previously mentioned various sunlight experiences. Many of the images seem so incredible. Some might even wonder if the photos had been enhanced. Not so though. One exception though is the image of Mt Warning with a small cloud atop its peak. The image needed different colours to give the proper authenticity to that photo's sun's rays emanating from the cloud and travelling outwards and upwards.

The chosen career/vocation choice to teach and to specialise in teaching religion eventuated in forty-two years of teaching religion in religious schools. Needing, but also strongly desired, to start each school day and each religion lesson with some communication with God is incredibly empowering. Class prayer and meditation was highly significant for all these years. For thirty of these years, the academic Study of Religion classes for years eleven and twelve required not just the spiritual dimension but the academic dimension. This subject needed an intimate knowledge and considerable experience, if possible, of the various religions of Christianity, Islam, Judaism, Buddhism, Hinduism and Australian Indigenous Spirituality. Teaching religion on these multiple levels every working day for such an extended time develops a genuine spiritual relationship with God. A truly loving relationship with the Divine! Your day is so much God-based. You truly get to appreciate God from each religion's perspectives and beliefs. Combine this with your own daily prayerful and meditative relationship with God, and a teacher of religious faith has something exceptional and unique from which to share.

Senior leadership positions in schools and parishes help with developing your relationship with God. These positions resulted from the personal, academic background being based on

Theology, Scripture, Liturgy and Religious Education, from experience gained in schools and through the personal spirituality being shared. Each qualification up to a master's degree has considerable levels of religion covered. Whether you are leading a school as principal or leading the religious aspect of the religious school as an assistant principal or senior school levels as a Year Coordinator, you should exemplifying and living your relationship with God, your faith and beliefs. You are challenged daily with everyday human aspects of others' relationship with God, religion, the religious school, etc. Through all this, your relationship with God grows and strengthens.

Senior parish roles result in similar experiences to the religious school but on a parish or deanery level. A deanery is a geographical grouping of various local parishes. It is led by the leadership priest who is known as a Dean. In my roles of Chair or Secretary of the parish or deanery pastoral councils place you as a non-clergy leader, primarily of both the service and visionary aspects. You are there to help facilitate the spiritual, religious and pastoral growth of members of your parish or deanery, also, as a laity help for the priests. Through experiencing the challenges and best of all these people you deal with through these roles, you cannot help but be strongly influenced by their challenges, successes and failures in life and their relationships with God and each other. The influence this has on strengthening your relationship with God is substantial.

When you have an authentic, prayerful relationship with God, so much of God's truth becomes apparent for the faithful. The impact is positively life-changing. You so much trust in God. God helps you through good and bad times. You have genuine compassion and empathy for humanity. God is indeed central to your existence.

The commandment by God about placing 'Him' as Number One across all genuine religions becomes real and actual. You then naturally aim to love each other as God does. It is through this prayer, meditation and action for God's lifestyle (as exemplified by Jesus, God Incarnate) that you are more open to God and more prepared to discern God's messages for yourself and others. Discernment of God's Words becomes not just real, but an essential part of your life.

Karen, my wife of forty-two years, this year, is integral to my relationship with God. Karen adds a depth needed to encounter God in these unique

> ...the need to accept my place in the scheme of God's plan and to go and do whatever is required to propagate the Revelation or message!
>
> ... Each of these ten reasons (p.111ff) supports the belief in the Revelations and inspired messages being from God.
>
> As do the following explanations in this article.

ways. She helps me understand and appreciate God's messages and Revelations through her unwavering support and openness to discuss each moment, each experience, each Tear from God encounter. And to share her contacts with God, often as the necessary support for my interaction with God!

(Edited Extract from *Where's God? Revelations Today,* by Bryan Foster, 2018, p. 39-45.)

Tears from God

My 'Road to Emmaus' experience, my epiphany, the 'Commitment to God' day on my 25th birthday, highlighted something extraordinary from God. (See Appendix 5)

It became evident to me, that when God wanted me to know something exceptional was coming from God, there would be a passing on of the Tears from God. These are not God's tears physically, but these are tears from God spiritually, which I experience physically, emotionally and spiritually.

There is an overwhelming sense of God's love and presence being intimately experienced at that moment. Words cannot describe what is happening, as it is very obvious to the recipient that it is on another level beyond the physical. Tears pour out in free-flow. There is no everyday contorted facial expressions or sobbing, as is typically associated with crying. It isn't crying as we know it, but tears are flowing uncontrollably.

Many others also experience these Tears from God. No one religion can claim this existence solely, as it occurs across several religions. This section mainly looks at the place of the tears in Christianity, Islam and Hinduism.

Just as these tears overwhelmed me all those years ago, each time God needs me to realise that something extra special is happening, or that differentiation is necessary between the things of this world and the things God wants me to know about or do, or that I need strong support as part of God's plan, God shares the Tears.

Many will say that this is all just emotion and that the tears come because I am emotional about something. Early on, this was my thought too. However, over time, there has developed a clear appreciation of the difference between normal emotional tears and those from God.

The difference is tough to explain, other than to say that the recipient gets this inherent feeling at the same time as the Tears that God is making it known that God is uniquely present at that moment. It is not just like *feeling* God's presence but *knowing* God is present.

Sometimes you almost hear words from God, but you know these are your words being inspired by God. (See Mt Warning story Appendix 2) Many people would appreciate this from their own prayer life when messages come to them from God. It is God's inspiration but through your thoughtful words.

These Tears from God were called on several times, as I went through the development of these books. I needed to be continually reminded that the Revelations and inspired messages of the books were correct. In *1God.world: One God for All* it was especially needed for the central premise and Revelation being unconditionally accepted before it was published: that there is only one God for all religions, peoples and cultures - forever. As well, all the inspired messages within the book up until the Mt Warning Revelation experience had been discerned as correct over several decades, yet reassurance through the Tears from God was still needed before publication. Similar support and verification from God were required for the next books, *Where's GOD: Revelations Today (2018)*, *Jesus and Mahomad are God (2020)* and *Love is the Meaning of Life: GOD's Love* (2020/1) with the publication of the Revelations and inspired messages contained within.

With the initial planning done in May 2016 for the first book, it was time to get God's approval. I stood with my wife, Karen, in our kitchen one evening and let her know I wasn't sure of the central premise for publication being singled out and emphasised, as I hadn't had any confirmation message from God. I was concerned that I might have been over-stepping the mark. At that moment, a rush of tears filled my eyes – Tears from God answered my call! The message from God was palpable - that it was correct and to go ahead, write the book and publish.

Since that time, there have been various other occasions when this assurance has been given, especially at Mt Warning. One particular example evolved into a video of this topic being recorded with Mt Warning as a background. **

I realise many people will challenge my belief in this. However, all I can say is that I inherently know it is correct and that I have God's support and encouragement to state this publicly and emphatically. (See also the 'Revelations and Inspired Messages from God' Appendix 1, p.265ff and 'Are the Revelations…the Truth from God?' p.110ff)

Let us consider where the Tears from God historically come from when considered in the three example religions of Christianity, Islam and Hinduism.

Christianity has long believed in this phenomenon with it often being referred to as the 'gift of tears' from the Holy Spirit (God). The Holy Spirit freely gives the charismatic gifts. Ewing beautifully encapsulates the closeness with God caused by these tears when she highlights how the Holy Spirit is infused into the receiver's soul. The action of the tears is the physical sign and personal experience of this bringing about such a result. The person will often be unable to explain what is or has happened - that the experience is somewhat subconscious and in a different realm.

Fenelon states how Pope Francis refers to these as 'the gift of tears'. He emphasises how this helps prepare the receiver to see Jesus (God), and how the concept is based on the 'Spiritual Exercises' of St Ignatius, especially where Ignatius is overwhelmed by the consolation of God. The Tears are coming from a sense of deep intimacy with God, primarily while Ignatius celebrated the Eucharist in all its beauty and presence of God's love. She goes on to share theologian Tim Muldoon's thoughts on how the pope sees this as a mystical experience of a deep, preconscious conviction of God's presence. It results from an overwhelming experience of receiving God's intimate love which can only be expressed through the free-flowing tears.

Fr Bartunek, who was an evangelical Christian and now a Catholic priest, explains that this gift can occur singularly or on multiple occasions. He states that it doesn't mean the receiver is any holier or any closer to God than others. He says it is an event to encourage those receiving or witnessing it to be in more significant and more substantial relationships with God. It provides excellent comfort from God, or confirming decisions which they had previously made, as well as a defence against temptation.

Physiologically Bartunek notes how these Tears from God are not like healthy tears resulting when someone is sobbing due to normal life's emotions. Still, these tears flow abundantly and freely without any physical tension or facial contortions. He also mentions that this gift isn't in scripture or the Catechism but has been referred to by various spiritual writers ever since the beginning of the early church.

In Al-Islam, examples of Tears from God are seen in both the Qur'an and traditions. Some examples in the Qur'an include when tears occur as a sign of perceiving the realities of God or as a sign of wisdom. Prophets shed tears for Allah when hearing of communications from God.

Tears are seen as so significant in Islamic tradition that they are a gift to humanity, illuminate and soften the heart and bring about a great reward from God, including extinguishing God's wrath.

Rattner speaks of what he calls the emotion of devotion, a crying for God, which he explores from both the Hindu and Christian traditions. Similar to both the Christian and Islamic examples above, the tears come from God at those special and often unique transformational moments with God. These were regular and spontaneous, purifying him to experience higher states of consciousness, leading to his continual spiritual development.

** See 'Tears from God…' video at https://www.youtube.com/watch?v=z5mmNvIKko4

(Edited Extract from *Where's God? Revelations Today,* by Bryan Foster, 2018, p. 46-50.)

Tears from God

There is an overwhelming sense of God's love and presence being intimately experienced at that moment.

Words cannot describe what is happening… it is on another level beyond the physical.

It is not crying or sobbing as we know it, but tears incredibly, lovingly, flowing uncontrollably -

Tears from God.

Is the Author a Prophet?

Would an author who claims to be a prophet be of assistance or a hindrance for you, the reader in a messed up, crazy world in which we live? Do you think a modern-day prophet is possible? If so, could they espouse various Revelations and inspired messages from God? Would you believe them, if they could explain why and how they are speaking the Truth from God? How would that help you in life, challenges, love and death? Are you a prophet?

Let's say that God requested a person to be a prophet, what would this mean, and how would it occur? We must be fully aware that God can do anything out of love, at any time, in any place, for whatever valid reason God so chooses! If the person requested by God agrees and does precisely as God requires, that is, in the case of this Book, promulgating the specific 21 Revelations, then the person very well may be a prophet of God!

What is a prophet? A prophet is someone selected by God to promulgate God's

Revelations, inspired messages and Absolute LOVE to an often-divided world.

As an example, let us consider the Catholic Church's teaching on prophets today. Prophets do exist today through the Baptism they teach. Many people worldwide will be called by God to promulgate and educate others on what are God's needs for them at various times throughout their lives. (As noted in the National Catholic Reporter. See https://www.ncronline.org/blogs/peace-pulpit/everyday-prophets-are-our-midst)

Beforehand, the person was usually a faithful follower of God. *It probably seems to be just as confusing or challenging for the person chosen to be the prophet, as for the community and others to accept this development.* The choice is incredibly significant for a new prophet because this person must be willing to take substantial risks in being prepared for the dissemination and then to disseminate the actual Word of God, to various groups. Some of the faithful, others and multiple groups will be very supportive, others not so - no matter what the answer is to this most incredible, introductory question.

Whether being a prophet today is true or not? Whether my wife or I believe it or not? Accepting that I am possibly a prophet is the most challenging reality for both of us, and I would imagine many others worldwide, as well.

So where do I think I fit in this prophetic situation? There are so many questions. It seems as if I may be a prophet, going by the Revelations as transcribed by me from God. This statement *"I am a prophet Prophets are true"* is firmly positioned on the bottom right corner of the first page of the two pages of Revelations dictated by God and transcribed by me? This was where God wanted the statement positioned. (See the list of the first 15 Revelations' from God in 2016 at p.134ff) But it is slightly away from the actual list of Revelations, on the right not the left side, like all the others asked to be written down by God. A personal Revelation one would imagine none-the-less - God specifically asking me this question. The Tears from God response answered seemed to answer this question unequivocally, YES! But?!

From my understanding, very few if any people seriously ask to be a prophet. Most prophets don't have it easy. Most prophets are just normal regular faithful followers of God, who are offered this incredible opportunity to talk/write for God and by God to God's people, and all others alike. I would imagine that such an invitation would challenge many people for many different reasons. Many of us would know what sort of recognition many people would 'cop' if they advised others of their Prophetic status - probably ranging from not very favourable, as has been the typical case throughout history, up to ecstatic joy. But, it is necessary to pass on whatever God wants passed to humanity to know at that time in history!

Going forward, please bear with me. What follows is the most challenging and complex statement I have ever had to acknowledge and state in my over sixty years of life. The initial reaction is to either disbelieve it or ignore it and go on.

This caused a massive conundrum. It was born as a centrepiece on the May, 2016 Revelations' list. While writing everything God passed to me verbatim, of the first 15 Revelations for this era of today, there was the prophet claim written separately at the bottom of the first page -

("I am a prophet Prophets are true" - Exact quote, minimal punctuation used as per 'God's Words'. Written here with the words and punctuation the same as it was at the time and a part of the Revelations in 2016. Italics is added now for highlighting the quote.)

Since that time and until this year, surprisingly, it didn't hold any attraction for me. It may seem strange, but I hardly noticed it until earlier in 2019. The most challenging decision was to acknowledge that *God had requested something significantly different than I had ever would have imagined.* I think that I would have loved to ignore it, deny it or just plead ignorance. However, this isn't how it's done. God asked something challenging for me. This spiritual/divine offer so humbled me! Tears from God flowed very freely and proved the Truth of these challenges. It was real!!!

After much deliberation, prayer and discussion with Karen, we decided I had to accept this request from God because it was a real, genuine, authentic request FROM GOD – I had just to do it!!!

It was an absolute honour and extremely humbling to receive such an invitation from God.

Whether I am a prophet or not doesn't stop me from revealing the 21 Revelations from God for today's world.

This is no doubt going to be for me, and I would expect for many others also, one of two of the most challenging aspects received as part of the Revelations from God in 2016 and 2018. Could my receival from God of the various prophecies /doctrines/commands, including that according to the Revelations' written by me from God, that I 'maybe' a modern-day prophet, and the promulgation of these, dictate the possibility that

I am an actual modern prophet? This is yet to be seen if it is the case either way. The good news is that nothing hangs on this explanation, no matter whether I am or not!

"Oh, yeah!?" I 'may hear' some of the readers say. "You can't be serious?! Who do you think you are? Why you?" etc.

I guess you could also ask, "Why not???"

God can do anything, Godly/Divinely! God's choices can be anything good! Obviously, God can ask anyone to do anything God wants to be done!

This then becomes quite challenging, if the author may be a possible modern-day prophet, is he one? Does it matter, as long as God's Revelations are passed on to the world?

So true. Precisely as we thought when finally confronted with this quote on Easter Eve 2019, in that it had no bearing on me until the Easter weekend in 2019, almost three years since receiving the majority of the Revelations, and then it happened.

While cooking our Saturday night BBQ, this message overawed me; especially as it seemed to come out of nowhere. The words from the 2016 Revelations' page kept repeating in my psyche.

> *And then the question of all questions came from the depths of my whole being -*
>
> *"Are you prepared to be a prophet for me [God]?"*
>
> *Tears from God immediately followed this question. It was indeed a request from God as per such criteria noted in a few of this Series' books. It was not forced, not coerced. Just a quiet yet strongly felt request! Karen (my wife) witnessed this Tears from God event as it occurred.*

An offer three years in the coming! (Wonder why I ignored/didn't realise/got lost in the whole prophet situation?!)

An offer fully and unconditionally accepted, while it was finally taken in and considered very seriously. The Tears from God was the tell-tail sign of its authenticity. Hence, I have no reason not to believe it. Can anyone ignore God's requests, especially when so much is placed on the Revelations from God?

When you know within your soul of souls and heart of hearts, this to be true, using all those points of proof about God and God's existence discussed in this book and others within this Series, you 'must' act! Free Will from God allows you to choose either way.

I believe the need to accept God's request. When it is so obviously placed and written on the bottom of page one of the two pages, surely it must be genuine. Being from God, it should be accepted; otherwise, you are ignoring something exceptional for you from God! It is believed that you would need to have some incredibly significant reason not to accept a personal, powerful, honest and truthful request coming from the creator of everything, everywhere for everybody!

Over these past four years (as of May 2016) since first receiving the initial Revelations, I have grown much closer to God, to the Revelations and God's place in our world. To now *accept unconditionally without questioning all the Revelations and Inspired Messages I have received from the One and Only God of eternity.*

The next most important question from me was, what am I supposed to do as a prophet, (if I am one)? Who do I tell and when? What needs promulgating? How do I promulgate what needs promulgating – so to speak?

I now know there was a learning curve for me to understand all this and to come to a fuller appreciation of this whole process and expected outcomes. So far, my belief is that I have been required to write about and then publish twelve of the Revelations received in 2016. To then do the same for the next nine, three of these were received in 2016, and another six were received in November, 2018. The *'GOD Today' Series* is very important and needs continual development from the books' publication options, the websites' perspectives, as well as the social media platforms, etc.

(Websites are *JesusAndMahomadAreGod.com* *GodTodaySeries.com,* and *BryanFosterAuthor.com* Social media at this stage is primarily Facebook at *'God Today'*. Other platforms will be developed over time.)

God has been guiding me with what and when to write and publish. At this stage, as I work on both *'GOD Today' Series* Books 5 and 7 simultaneously, the timeline becomes more apparent. The last book for this series is now planned to be released in 2020/1/2. (Coincidentally, numerically 2020 could be astrologically, theologically and numerically 'played' with and be 20+20, which equals 40.

This number 40 is a very significant number for various religions, for example, Christianity, Judaism, and Islam and often stands for developing purity and perfection while growing closer to God. Christian examples such as Jesus' 40 days in the desert, the 40 days from the resurrection of Jesus until His Ascension to Heaven, (Taylor, 2016). The three religions have Moses leading his people for 40 years wandering the desert before reaching the Promised Land. Islam also has Moses spending 40 days on Mt Sinai to receive the 10 Commandments. Forty years of age is sometimes seen as the length of time for people to reach their intellectual and cognitive appreciation of life entirely. There are other examples of a remarkable 40 for these religions.

Expert groups of theologians, scriptural scholars and other leaders and scholars from many religions, now need to pray, consult, reflect and discern on these latest Revelations from God. Maybe there could even be more Revelations received by others, which should be included here? And then to explain how these may help our troubled world.

It is then up to us all to implement the findings.

I sense very strongly that four of the Revelations will indeed be quite challenging for many, if not most people. All I can do is invite everyone to seriously be open to God's Absolute Love and invitation for us to do what needs to be done at this time in history. Are we prepared to take up this invitation?

It is essential to realise the significance of all this for humanity. Our cultures and histories are now at a crossroads. There are a few directions we could take, and must choose between, right now, A.S.A.P.!

So, am I a prophet?

I honestly believe that God has asked me to be a prophet, through the written word and divine thoughts encouraged by God to me in 2016. God will not apply any force on me to make this significant decision - out of Absolute Love.

I have no magical powers to predict the future. Yet, I have received Revelations, Inspired Messages and religious discernment from God over the decades, especially these recent five years. This is also possible for other people worldwide. God has 'spoken' to me in a variety of ways about what to pass onto our world through this book's *Series*. I firmly believe that writing this *Series* of seven or eight books on God could not have been done otherwise. God has strongly guided this *Series'* publication's content and processes.

It certainly appears to support the possibility being considered. I feel a genuine part of this offer. I appreciate what God wants to be done. It seems to have been genuine when I was aware of it being offered both from the written word and Tears from God. Karen, my wife, witnessed the Tears example.

I believe that my humanity should allow me to make this decision out of Free Will. If not, I do believe that God can. After all, God can do anything God wants to do.

So basically, I don't know if I am a prophet?

Even though so much points to this conclusion, including a written statement on the original 15 Revelations pages, plus God's request of me at home with Karen.

I feel a lot closer to a decision, though, having completed this Book 5.

I do know that God wants me to write and communicate through a variety of modern-day ways about all these experiences. To invite all people through the written Word for them to become once more as close as possible with God.

I tend to think and feel the certainty of being a part of this prophetic role isn't too far away. This honoured role from God is more than likely being offered to other believers also.

God has strongly guided this *Series'* publications' content and processes…

It seems to have been genuine when I was aware of it being offered both through the written Word and the Tears from God…

Karen witnessed the Tears…

So basically I don't know the answer yet???

I do know that God wants me to write and communicate. I also seem to feel a strong calling to be a part of this honoured role for God…

As far as I can tell, God has asked me to be a prophet, through the written Word and Divine Thoughts (Inspired Messages)…

I have received Revelations, Inspired Messages and religious discernment from God over the decades, especially these recent five years…

So Is being a prophet true? Yes, if that's what God wants.

COVID-19 Costs and Military Costs

If the author is a prophet (?), it is one of the author's roles to promulgate as much of God's Wisdom and Love as possible to the world's populations. This new virus, still without a vaccine discovered yet (in July – at the time of writing this article), appeared on the world stage in 2019/20. It has caused millions to be sick, with hundreds of thousands to die, so far.

There are now two other situations developing. Both are economical and will have significant impacts on the world and specific places/countries within the world. The Covit-19 virus has forced many countries to act excessively with monetary solutions to assist the medical teams and facilities, e.g. hospitals, the unemployed, the commercial world, the public works, etc. The cost is in the billions up to hundreds of billions at this stage for each affected country, making such a commitment.

As politicians and many others keep stating that the world will change due to this virus, it will also include changes to the impacted economies for both the virus and associated billions of dollars, plus what is possibly also becoming apparent. There will perhaps be military costs associated with realigning countries or threatened or scaring these with military might and bad diplomacy. *These military positionings could quite quickly end in either a hot or cold war occurring over many years.*

The world has already defeated a cold war in the middle of the last century, which ran for decades, as the more significant, wealthy countries kept building military equipment, especially nuclear bombs in their tens of thousands worldwide. It developed a fear of atomic devastation for any country considering to start a nuclear war. Hence, it stopped a hot war. Could we successfully survive another cold war if it eventuated? Where's God in our plans? Have we turned to God for assistance? If not, why not? We must believe in God's Absolute Love and turn to God in times of crises – NOW!.

On a significant worldwide medical/health issue, the COVID-19 /Coronavirus pandemic is so far afflicting and impacting upon millions of people worldwide. At the time of writing, the virus needs urgent solutions! A vaccine seems to be the greatest need according to the medical experts – time will tell. *This is a particular time to call on God through prayer for urgent assistance.* We may or may not have the ability to use science to discover and develop the vaccine ourselves as a world population. It requires a vaccine for a virus! No vaccine exists for a viral cold. Is the COVID-19 vaccine possible or impossible? *We might need a much higher level of assistance – GOD!*

Personal and communal prayer to God over whatever time we need, (only time will tell in hindsight), will add a considerable depth of engagement with God. This could lead to solutions being found and acted upon earlier and better than anticipated. *That is up to God. Often we can't understand God's choices, but we need to acknowledge the possibilities, support God's judgments, and not put God to the test*! But don't ever give up on God!

The other monetary situation involves hundreds of millions of dollars, or even trillions of dollars, revolving around various countries feeling the pressure to defend themselves against known or unknown but suspected countries. The military levels and hence costs will increase enormously in trying to calm and stop the aggressive countries from attacking others.

All this money will need to be paid back by countries with deficits to other countries, banks or other institutions, etc.

There appears to be beginning a realignment of various countries worldwide. Some countries are feeling more threatened than ever. The three largest economies and military powers will have huge impacts on this threat. If we don't end up with a cold war, a hot war could be threatened and maybe eventuate.

It appears that the western world is slowly losing its belief in prayer; this could be a most remarkable time to 'reboot' our God relationships. Growing closer to God can only help in our time of urgent need.

The primary questions and choices right now are – are we with God, against God, or undecided on God? We must grow closer to God, *accepting that we always need God's help*. It is not in reality, optional. That is our duty as loving humans. Otherwise, *this will impact on lifestyle choices now and/or choices at death.*

What will it take for us to make the right decisions about God – now!? Why? So that we may continually grow closer to God and be with God for our human lifetimes. Until finally being with God in Heaven. The other incredibly difficult challenge though is Revelation #15 (See p.90ff, p.181ff)

Expert combined groups of religious leaders, theologians, scriptural scholars and others from Christianity, Islam, Judaism and Hinduism, possibly along with other authentic religions, need to pray, consult, study, reflect, research and discern these latest Revelations from God.

And explain to all humanity in non-complicated languages what these are and how these may help a troubled world.

One God
Two
Incarnations

Bryan Foster

Jesus and Mahomad are both the Incarnate GOD - in different eras

One God - Two Incarnations - Overview

The following revealed/discerned detail for the Revelations from God in this next section was received in Australia in 2016. It was seen as inspired messages and written in Canada in 2018 and completed in Australia in 2019. The initial draft pages were written in Vernon, BC, Canada during October 2018 and finished on the Gold Coast in Australia in 2020. This timeline is from God.

This Revelation is broken up into some specific vital concepts and explanations in line with God's Revelation #15.

These key aspects follow:

One God

One God - Two Incarnations

How on earth could this be possible?

The Time is Now!

Science and Technology – God's Gifts

World, it is time to face reality

Revelation #15

God Calls Religious Leaders to Act

One God

The One God Revelation in this collection of Revelations received by the author is in line with the original theme of this *'GOD Today' Series* - the emphasis is on there being *Only One God for all religions for all time, forever.* Book 1 highlighted and developed this belief and Revelation from God in 2016.

These final Revelations are significant, yet simply follow the themes of the previously listed and discussed 12 Revelations received by the author in May 2016. The first 12 were listed in the first four books of the series and explained in detail in Book 3, *Where's God? Revelations Today.*

These last Revelations emphasise the earlier 'One God only – One God' Revelation and link the significant four world religions of Christianity, Islam, Hinduism and Judaism. The One God only is explicitly listed as Jesus, Brahma/n, Yahweh, Allah.

"Jesus is God. Yahweh is God. Allah and Mahomad are God. Brahma/n is God."

(Summary of Revelation #15, p53ff, p.90ff, p.181ff)

Many people would have little difficulty accepting that this 'God' is, or at least could be, the One and Only God of all time. It is the firm belief of the author that God has spoken specific Revelations to him stating this explicitly, i.e. 'One God only – One God'. Reasons for this belief are detailed in Books 1 and 3, *1God.world: One God for All* and *Where's God? Revelations Today*.

People of the world are now challenged to accept that there truly is only One God for all people, religions and cultures, forever.

This is a much-freeing appreciation of the reality of God. It requires no more literal and figurative fighting between religions and each religion's denominations.

People of the world

are now challenged

to accept that there truthfully is

Only One God for

all people,

all religions,

all cultures,

FOREVER!

+

2 Incarnations of GOD –

Jesus and Mahomad

One God - Two Incarnations

One God – Two Incarnations is the most challenging of all these Revelations today and will be most likely very difficult for many people to accept. Yet, *this Revelation was explicitly stated by God during the Revelations to the author in 2016.* Not only explicitly stated but *with the added directive from God to 'Don't doubt this'.* This book will be published in 2020, according to God's advice. Each book in the *'GOD Today' Series* has been published as per a timetable from God.

The challenge for the author is that it is so completely against everything he has been taught as a Christian and as a teacher of world religions. Neither of the two religions concerned, Islam and Christianity have ever, to his understanding, made these claims. Yet, these need to be made at the appropriate time as dictated by God.

As previously explained in Book Three, it has become apparent to the author that even though

God revealed the Revelations in 2016 (and 2018 after the publication of Book 3 and 4, too late to be included in those books), *there is an actual timeline on which God requires various Revelations to be published*. At this stage, the first two books emphasised that there is 'One God only – One God'. At the same time, twelve Revelations were detailed in Book 3, with Book 4 being a necessary companion to Book 3, especially on the author's relationship with God through highly supported photographic images. These sun images were explained in detail and photographically shown in this photobook Book Four. These should excite and assist the reader! Each is genuinely inspirational.

There are many exceptionally unique and necessary photographic GOD Signs in Book 4, *Where's GOD? Revelations Today Photobook Companion: GOD Signs*, which helps explicitly and inherently with Book 3, especially, and all the *Series'* other Books, as well. These images are fantastic - including sun arrows appearing across the author and his books, sun flares, double rainbows and cloud/sun rays above Mt Warning.

Very spectacular, yet challenging images. I believe the main reason for such photos is to inspire the writer and readers to accept these photos as genuine inspirations for us from God and to be authentically open to make clear to the world each Revelation received from God by the author in 1982, 2016 and 2018.

Book 3 and Book 4 are best read together as unique images help with God's contemporary-inspired messages in Book 3, considerably.

Book 4 is also best used in conjunction with all the Books of this *Series* due to its excellent and yet challenging images from God. Take your time exploring these images – the sun arrows can be missed if not concentrating on each photo, even though each is quite clear.

Book 5's theme is Incarnation, i.e. God becoming fully human – twice!!! As Jesus and Mahomad!

For over two thousand years, Christians have claimed that Jesus the Christ is the Incarnation of God. As a Christian, I wholeheartedly believe this intrinsically. However, no other religion accepts this belief fully. The best some other religions do is to either accept Jesus as a prophet, e.g. Islam and Judaism. Or, similarly to Christians, in Hinduism at his death, maybe Jesus became an enlightened one and merged with the Godhead.

With these most recent Revelations from God, God goes that next step.

God became a fully complete human in the form of Jesus and Mahomad at two critical times in history that we are now aware of so far. So around 500 years after Jesus returned as God in Heaven, He returned to be Mahomad for the Muslims.

This is not a threat to Islam or Christianity in any way what-so-ever! It is a Revelation which enhances and depths both these religions. Both religions need to show considerable maturity as they develop the necessary theologies and teachings, etc. *The author of this book is not qualified to be an academic researcher or biblical scholar, etc.* He is a conduit from God to the religions of today. The full Truth needs to come from religious leaders, theologians, scriptural scholars, etc. Especially from both Islam and Christianity, but also any other interested, genuine religions, particularly Judaism and Hinduism who also only believe in one God.

> God's revealing of these at this time in history to the author, shows that humanity is now ready to receive the latest
> 21 Revelations – esp. incl. the Two Incarnations of GOD!

How on Earth could this be possible?

The actual response is quite simple: why couldn't it be so? The One and Only God of the universe of all time and for all creation - can do anything good/GODLY!

But what of the previous teachings and patterns of doctrine and beliefs over millennia? How can these change? We need to consider that each has developed forward as well as changing. 1400-2000 years is very considerable. Much can improve over this time. *God is now telling us that the time has come for critical developments within these two specific religions, the largest two throughout the world.*

Once the perspective of there being only one God for all people and religions for all time is accepted, the apparent 'block' or reticence to compare various religions' beliefs and practices needs to be eliminated. The first book in this series, *1God.world: One God for All,* considered the

One God only for all time, and all people, in detail.

From this day forward, in the first instance, Christians, Muslims and probably Hindus and Jews, in particular, need to work very closely together to gain a fuller more complete appreciation of these Incarnations of the One and Only - God.

There will be those who argue that, at times, the ethics of both Jesus and Mahomad are quite different, particularly with regards to the place of violence.

There will be those who very strongly argue that it is anathema to make such Incarnate claims about Mahomad. Islam's particular view of God is that Allah is God and Mahomad is the prophet but not God. These have been the principal beliefs of Islam since Mahomad's days.

Each is a significant belief and must be fully respected by all involved – i.e. Islamic faithful and as many other religions as possible. The premise is different for different religions. The main reason that I am sharing this with the whole world is that God has asked me to do it. And I answered, "Yes!" All after considerable Revelations from God, prayer, meditation, discernment and time with God.

There will be those who argue that, at times, the ethics of both Jesus and Mahomad are quite different, particularly with regards to the place of violence.

There will be those who very strongly argue that it is anathema to make such Incarnate claims about Mahomad.

Yet God has revealed these to us in our era.

The Time is Now! We're all in this together.

It is now the era for all religions to finally come together and discover how these claims can be so for everyone and every authentic religion.

The 'why' I believe, has already been answered – there is Only One GOD forever!

God is calling on all people to engage with one another to bring humankind together.

Of course, it will not be easy! Of course, it will be a significant change for many, if not most – *but it is time!!! It's God's time!!!*

People have to stop fighting and arguing about religious beliefs and practices. Stop the claims of salvation being only for their devout followers.

In the cyber-global-world of today, most things are possible. We now have the technology to make many remarkable beliefs and teachings happen. Things never before thought of as possible. We can certainly bring people together far more successfully than ever before – primarily through the cyber world and its various, necessary, digital technology.

The only things which will hold us up from delivering God's Revelations to a divided world will be the prejudices, mistrust and even hate various people, societies and religions espouse or believe of others.

The world needs to be very open to real religious changes in our time without the loss of significant beliefs and teachings of other times and other religions. Necessary additions and developments of these new and historical Revelations, along with the unique and inspiring God signs, continue our journey to God and salvation.

IT'S TIME!!! WE MUST DO IT!!!

Bryan Foster

It's time for people to stop believing that only they or their religion/group have the answers, whether religious or secular. The world is at the most challenging crossroads.

> **It is now the era for all authentic religions to finally come together and discover how all of these 21 Revelations, plus Inspired Messages can be so for everyone and every religion.**

Our Response to God

This is how we must react and respond to our GOD, as discovered through the previous explained 21 Revelations:

1. We must accept who we are and where we are on this divine continuum. We must recognise that we have the credentials and skills to meet and greet every person who has an interest, no matter how small, in God and faith, wherever they may be in their relationships with God and others.

2. We must show absolute vulnerability to our MOST LOVING GOD. No heroics, grandstanding or claiming to be on a higher level with God than anyone else does. Be meek, humble and real. These are the valued characteristics of God for us.

3. Claim our True Love for GOD! When we can authentically claim a loving relationship with God without any prerequisites or false claims, we can then develop this loving relationship with God and with humanity.

4. A love where we don't question, put on trial or challenge!

God Directs Us

1. We must accept that we are dependent on God for everything!

2. Yes, we have Free Will and an informed conscience to decide, yet God is there for us on every occasion we have – no matter how good or bad!!!

3. For every day, hour, minute and second of our existence.

4. We live on a knife's edge, where anything could go right or wrong or change at any time!

5. We need God to guide and direct us accordingly out of God's Absolute Love for us all - equally.

6. All people are invited to become a part of Heaven on Earth throughout their earthly lives. Live as truthfully and lovingly as Jesus lived. And finally, at death, become a full member of Heaven, itself. To go on to exist for all time with all people who are accepted there, entirely in absolute love with our absolutely loving God and absolutely loving people.

7. Only the perfect will enter Heaven. Time may be needed after death to develop perfection, though. Everyone will be given a choice at death, as to where to go. Then it's up to us individually.

Science and Technology – God's Gifts

Science and technology are God's gifts to us, so that we can understand God and creation and for humanity to then use this knowledge to make the world a better place for everyone.

Don't think that today's technology was some hit and miss experience of some fortunate scientists. There is undoubtedly an aspect of this in any scientific discovery, yet we need to accept the guidance God has given these people along the way. We, as humans, are not alone. We are guided by a supreme force – the creator of the universe - GOD.

Can anyone honestly believe that the universe and everything in it is an accident? Fell into existence on its own. Yes? - but NO WAY!

God loves science and technology. The scope it offers is for people to gain a much more informed and safer place with understanding God's creation. *It is one of the profound gifts from God for humanity.* Once humanity appreciates God's creation, they are then able to move forward, using their newly discovered scientific findings to create and build an enhanced and more equal world for all.

Science is God's Gift to humanity for the sake of humankind. *It is up to those with specialised scientific knowledge and skills, to work with religious academics, theologians and religious leaders, etc. to bring God's absolute, loving, desires for us – much closer!* We need these people to help us all to understand and appreciate God in all God's forms and ways.

> Science and technology are God's gifts
>
> to help us understand God and creation
>
> and for humanity to then use this knowledge
>
> to make the world a better place for everyone.

Revelation #15

Revelation #15 from God to the author in May 2016

Jesus is God [**]

Brahma(/n) is God

Yahweh is God

Mahomad/Allah is God [**]

Mahommad is Allah is God.

Jesus and Mahamod is God.

[*] Don't doubt this.

Double Asterix stands for the joining of these two Revelations with lines as on the written initial Revelations, i.e. join the two written lines beginning with 'Jesus' and 'Mahomad'. Plus, the instruction to not doubt these two lines' authenticity.

Spelling and punctuation are exactly as written at the Revelation.

Revelation #15 – the Detail – Jesus and Mahomad are God

Revelation #15 is, I believe, the major Revelation from the original series of Revelations revealed in May 2016. Until now, it was not mentioned, being so as requested by God until the appropriate time. The timeline from God, which I was advised of from God, now places this book as the Fifth Book in the *'GOD Today' Series* – no longer Book 7.

The time is now right to spread this –

most wonderful teaching from God.

This book is the first publication worldwide of Revelation #15, of that I am aware.

Readers are asked to respect this publication of the Revelation from God. The release will no doubt cause considerable discussion, acceptance or denial, and possibly some readers will be overcome by emotion and even some possible grief to its Truth and place in our religious world.

Please remember that this is:

a Revelation from God, which is the Truth, and needs to be acted upon now, truthfully and respectively.

No violence is acceptable. This is a purely violence-free promulgation by our loving and absolutely peaceful God of ALL! Criminal violence will show the evil of the perpetrators. God rarely accepts violence - it is evil. Only acceptable in self or communal defence as needed.

Anyone who concludes a need for violence BECAUSE OF Revelation #15 is so far away from what God wants from us!!! This genuine, authentic **Revelation #15 from God is real.** It is revealed to challenge us to develop a better world for all, no matter their religion, lifestyle, career, beliefs, etc.

Any violence resulting from this Revelation by any people will be seen by God as EVIL, with the appropriate response eventually forthcoming from God. No religion will honestly need to encourage the evil of violence after reading and analysing this Revelation. It is a beautiful Revelation for all!

Twelve possible critical outcomes, which could help us all achieve full acceptance of this Revelation, are worth considering:

1. God can do anything, at any time, involving anyone or anything so chosen.
2. God is divine and not physical, yet became Incarnate (physically fully human) twice in history - that we now know from these latest Revelations – God came as Jesus and Mahomad.
3. These Revelations were of Jesus approximately 2000 years ago and Mahomad around 1400 years ago becoming Incarnate of the one and only God of all time, of all people, of all religions.
4. God loves all people equally and wants each person to eventually become one again with God both here and in Heaven. Our response to God's absolute Love is what counts. If we freely choose against God, then what we do is evil. We do evil; God does not!!! God only Loves!
5. We have no right ever to challenge God about anything. *We need to fully and absolutely understand*

and practise where we as humankind fit in this relationship.

Good people are subservient to God always.

6. Many people find this imbalance too much of a challenge and go their own way - wrongly. Insolence is evil. People placing themselves equal to, or better than, God are evil – because they are going against God. That is what is EVIL!

7. **Even though many people will be challenged considerably by this Revelation #15, we must react peacefully, lovingly and explore what is being told about this Revelation. And how we can implement it as the Truth from our most Loving God.**

8. God has advised that the religious leaderships, theologians, scriptural scholars and others of the mainline monotheistic religions in particular (and other genuine religions wishing to be involved) need to research quickly, pray, discern etc. then explain and teach Revelation #15 and what its impact, etc., on the world as

a whole will be. Especially for the two religions directly involved, Christianity and Islam.

9. *Be it known and promulgated as quickly as possible, that:*

accepting this Revelation #15 will instigate an incredible wave of freedom and closeness with our God and each other for all those open to God's latest, essential Revelations.

10. This occurs because as a society, and not just as single religions, which often disagree or even fight or argue with each other on various levels, usually on the intellectual or physical levels, we must listen to God's latest Revelations. *These Revelations are The Truth.* These are true because God made it known that these were True Revelations passed on at God's direction?

11. *Just as Jesus is entirely accepted as God Incarnate by Christians, Mahomad now needs to be fully accepted as God Incarnate by Islam. This is God's main*

message for today. It is so essential that it is the title of this book.

12. As much as many may like to ridicule this new teaching, and the arrival of it so unexpectantly, for them directly from God in the present-day, they have no right legitimately do so. *It is evil to do so!* God has Revealed #15, and we as a world society and followers of various religions must accept it. *We have no right to argue or disagree, as that would be to challenge God, and that is never allowed!*

Any violence resulting from this Revelation will be seen by God/Allah as EVIL,

with the appropriate response eventually forthcoming from God.

No religion will honestly need to encourage the evil of violence after reading and analysing this Revelation.

It is a beautiful Revelation for all!

It's impact should be extra-special for humanity.

World, it is time to face reality!!!

All our false claims of human superiority, magnificence and ability to do anything we want are over. We can't do everything on our own. We are mere mortals living on a knife-edge. Can anyone honestly say they have the power to extend their lives even for one more minute if that is not God's Will? No. We might be able to improve our life's quality and hence our potential for more life, but if our timing is different to God's ultimate, it won't happen. Most people know of examples of the very fit and healthy individuals of most ages who just often die unexpectedly from illness, injury or self-infliction.

Life and death are so complex and complicated that except for some minor ability to extend life or its quality as humans, we have a minimal say in our lifespan.

Today's lifespan is an incredible advance on what it used to be only a few decades back and considerably less the further historically we go back. If we were to compare it to when Jesus and

Mahomad were Incarnate as humans, on average, we live decades longer now.

But the eternal question then becomes, are we living a quality life in our old age or state of illness etc. *or have we medically extended life's timeline well beyond what is best for us?!* Are we just inviting certain diseases and injuries to become more prevalent? For what reason, apart from living longer in the health state we are?

Therefore, the most significant reason to make this acceptance of actual reality and living the life where God is so superior to us and our mortality as being very limiting for us, we must accept that the challenge offered by God is also quite simple. Why and how?

Initially, God is not out there to trick us. Absolute Love for us doesn't allow for 'tricks'. We belong to God forever and therefore are strongly invited to believe, act and do as God instructs. Our teachers and preachers must communicate in clear, straightforward ways to allow everyone to appreciate what is needed from God and for each other.

All our false claims of human superiority, magnificence and ability to do anything we want are over – says God.

We can't do everything on our own. We are mere mortals living on a knife-edge.

…have we medically extended life's timeline well beyond what is best for us?!

…We belong to God forever. God created us, all of us!!!

…and therefore are strongly invited to believe, act and do as God instructs.

Be as Positive as You Can

God is permanently with us, waiting for our correct and best response to His invitation to love all, as much as God loves us individually and communally. We find the best explanations in the covenants and significant teachings of God historically for all genuine religions. *Reading God's Word in whatever texts, which belong to your particular religion, helps lead us to God and loving human relationships. Yet, with all the help and encouragement from God, so many people still ignore, disagree and fight against God's teachings. Even thinking that these make life boring, not fun, way too serious! And who are we to try and assist these people in seeing the Truth anyway?*

Yet, we also have much positivity about most people. We have been told and shown by God, what we must do for salvation. We know within our heart-of-hearts that love, hope and charity offer us so much while here on Earth. Have we heard God's invitations? Have we acted on those offerings to make ourselves and our world more loving, more hopeful and more charitable? Or have we just given up, or 'thrown our hands in the air' or decided it was way too much and way too difficult and hence ignored it, denied it, rejected it. *God is 'desperately' wanting us to make the right choices and actions so that we can eventually spend eternity with God in Heaven.*

Why do people try and push God away, because doing what is Godly/goodly is best for everyone, and commanded by God? Why do people overreact against God when so many things are the result of other people's behaviour or decisions? Why argue against God's absolute Love and power and ignorantly reject such help as a sign of weakness – it is a strength to work with God and against evil people and hateful others.

It often appears as a cheap copout by these deniers and selfish individuals to accept minimal or no blame, and yet blame it on God. In western civilisations, people are commonly reacting against God and followers of God. These reactions are now growing among other second and third worlds also. God can never, by definition, do anything wrong! Everything God does is good for us (somehow) even though we may not understand why at that stage? Time will tell why it positively happened.

It will all happen when God so chooses.

> God makes everything very clear to anyone who wants to know.
>
> God is not out there to 'trick' us or make life too difficult.
>
> Absolute Love for us doesn't allow for 'tricks' and difficulties.
>
> We belong to God forever and therefore are strongly invited to believe, act and do as God instructs.
>
> Actively and honestly search for God in our lives.

GOD SAID TO FACE REALITY!

God says it is time.

God is here to guide us through the process.

All God needs is

US TO GENUINELY SAY YES BY OUR THOUGHTS AND ACTIONS!!!

Then be very open to what comes next from God.

Time isn't relevant.

God Calls Religious Leaders to Act

This most transforming Revelation #15 is now out there. It is the most critical Revelation of this Fifth Book and the *'GOD Today' Series.* It is time for our religious leaders to study this Revelation from God, pray, discern, accept its authenticity and to then justify it theologically for each religion's followers.

It will most likely require these religions working together very closely in ways never imagined! Something from which we should all benefit. Clarifying a common question and answer concept. *An essential core for both Christianity and Islam will be how to accept and teach that Jesus and Mahamod were both God Incarnate to this world,* but historically at different times and in similar geographic places.

Never before have our religious leaders and their advisers, scholars, etc. been required to explain why this Revelation #15 is correct - being a new

Revelation from God to our era and future, 2016 onwards.

They also need to explain what the outstanding ramifications for at least these two religions will be. There are also significant opportunities for other faiths to join in and have their discernments and studies shared. Along with other Revelations, they may want to consider seriously between religions and denominations. It mainly applies to Hinduism and the Hindu belief in the one and only God, Brahman and the millions of manifestations of Brahman. The other dominant monotheistic religion, Judaism, would also benefit from these divine Incarnations. How, you might ask? There would be a challenge to acknowledge that God was both Incarnate Jesus and Incarnate Mohamad. These two incarnations of God are not just to be seen as prophets once the researches and scholars etc. reach a conclusion and understand this Incarnate Revelation. This is mainly due to the closeness between each of these three, middle-eastern, monotheistic religions. Even the geographical proximity of their significant religious mosques, churches, temples and synagogues would assist with this significant challenge! Many beliefs are very similar and shared.

It is also a strong possibility that there will be considerable push back from the specific religions as a whole, or particular members and/or groups of each religion or society.

My role from God at this stage is to 'get these twenty-one Revelations promulgated' with a specific genuine push for Revelation #15.

And to advise the Scholars and Leaders of legitimate faiths to treat these as authentic from God and needing their considered, honest, opinions to be imparted to us all.

The push will come from this book, and other sources which may now exist, and from those faithful who, I would imagine, bravely support this specific Revelation. *Everyone who finally accepts this Revelation #15 is then called upon to assist in whatever way possible that they can.* To help make it real and genuine for all religions. It may arise through their religious studies, including their scriptural and theological studies, or their prayer life, or lifestyle, or their religious communities or academia, etc.

Placing all these 2016 and 2018 Revelations and inspired messages shared with the reader and any other writers from authentic religions' Revelations, on the table in 2020, is a crucial direction from God for all people.

Even though Revelation #15 is specifically for Christianity and Islam (and possibly Hinduism and Judaism), *all religions should benefit through a significant awakening of these essential Revelations and inspired messages from God.* These should impact all faiths due to the nature of this revelatory occurrence. Who is up for the challenge? Hopefully - the world!

Optimistically, to bring the world together for the first time in history through religions, religious beliefs and God's Revelations. The world needs to accept that God is so superior, so powerful, so loving, so gentle, so forgiving, so life-changing…

Hopefully, this would allow for all people to be represented at the table, at least indirectly through their religion. For the everyday followers of God, to finally have some say, whether highly qualified or not, is rewarding for the openness and loving support of the Truth from God. Literally from the bottom up, of *the laypeople having some input into what God desires for all people. Yet, respecting the leadership and scholarly groups to lead and guide people's reactions to these Revelations.*

The leadership powerbase still must rest with those particularly educated in religion, religious issues and theologies, etc., who must themselves *be open to developed or different Revelations or Inspired Messages from God and views and opinions from other religions and individual people.*

We are all Equal! There is ONLY ONE GOD for all people, of all religions, for all time!

God Calls Us All to Follow 'Him'

God calls us to 'Him' in so many different ways, depending on our interests, health, well-being, love, lifestyle, culture, religion and many more.

This *'GOD Today' Series* is currently at Book 5, *Jesus and Mahomad are God*. Each previous book highlights something else for us to challenge ourselves with and to get some serious Truths from God. This Book 5 is slightly different in that it assumes the reader either hasn't read the previous books or would like a summary of critical points of earlier books included here. Key topics are summarised, with a number set as appendices. Others appear positioned where they are needed.

See Books 1 and 3 of this series for specific details of the first twelve Revelations and six inspired messages from God.

See Books 2 and 4 for spectacular photos. Book 4, my favourite, will be quite challenging for many. Its images are very different from what is expected. Sun arrows and flares appear out of nowhere on or around me. The vast Easter Sun Cross appearing on the NSW side of Texas (on the Qld border) is exceptionally eyeopening. It is so spectacular that it is the cover image of Book 4. The small cloud atop of Mt Warning has rays of sunshine flowing out of it upwards and outwards.

As I was literally told by God when writing down the 21 Revelations highlighted in this Book 5, *'Don't overthink this. Just write it down."* I believe this same instruction is relevant for anyone viewing these images now. There may be a tendency for some to strike all this off as being way too unbelievable and being impossible!

But nothing is impossible for God, except evil! (God can not turn away from Himself, as we do from God when we sin.)

However, no matter what you or I think, these Revelations' images, and inspired messages from God are all so real!!! An excellent starting point for the reader is to read this book and others in the series and be very open to what is found. Accept these as the Truth and move forwards with God and with God's followers. I believe wholeheartedly that these Revelations are from God directly. Remember, *we can't challenge God or put God to the test!* Of course, *we can ask questions of God and be prepared for God's answers,* no matter how close or far away to what we expect these to be. *So it is the best opportunity to become one with God in love – open to real challenges and Godly support - loving, forgiving, being with God through our prayers and actions, and with the others, we come in contact with daily.*

Once taken on board, these aspects of God's Revelations and messages to us will become tremendous support for our search for God and God's place in today's world. And of God's place

> …it will be ideal if all genuine religions could engage with this crucial modern Revelation #15 – after all, it is from God for humanity.

with the reader and other interested people from around the world.

Never before have our religious leaders and their advisers, scholars, theologians etc. been required to explain why this Revelation #15 is correct - as it is a new God Revelation from our era - 2016.

They are also required by God to explain what the outstanding ramifications for at least these two religions, **Christianity and Islam**, will be. There is also room for other religions to join in…

Advised God

Bryan Foster

21 Revelations for Today

God's Revelations # 1-21

1. Be Truthful
2. Don't be Greedy
3. Love life – don't take it
4. Respect all
5. Love one another as I have loved you
6. **Die for what is right**
7. Be educated for what is right & truthful
8. Education is paramount for all
9. We are one -
10. One God only One God

("I am a prophet Prophets are true"???

This is the physical placement by number along with its punctuation in the Revelations received, i.e., after number ten and on the right lower side of the page.)

11. God's messages to a world in need
12. This world is in enormous need
13. Cyberbullying – in all its forms, of all sorts, of all ages.
14. Fear rules – often from the cyber world eliminate this
15. **God is Jesus & Mahomad***
16. We need God

17. We need <u>to be vulnerable to God</u>
18. We need to continually be asking for God's help and assistance & support – always. 'No big heads' – Just ask for help. Always.
19. We are insignificant compared to God
20. God is so superior – face up to it. Believe it! Stop fighting it!
21. Be meek & humble & real

(Revelations to the author in 2016 and 2018. Received at the base of Mt Warning, NSW, Australia, and written here correctly, as received from God.

These are not for any specific religion, yet Christianity and Islam are specially named for Revelation #15 due to its content.

However, these 21 Revelations are for all religions who follow our ONE GOD of all genuine and authentic faiths.

As well as the many others, who also want to accept this invitation to be fully involved.)

Revelations #1-15 from 28/29 May, 2016, were received on the plains at the foot of Mt Warning, Murwillumbah Showgrounds, NSW Australia after being awoken in the early hours of the morning around 3am while staying in my caravan/trailer.

Revelations #16-21 received at Mt Warning Rainforest Park at approximately 3 am on November 3, 2018.

The next few pages explain the discerned meaning of each of the last six Revelations, i.e., #16-21.

Latest Revelations #16-21

Two and one-half years after the first fifteen Revelations from God, another six were received. The revealing of both sets of Revelations from God occurred while I was initially asleep but was awoken during the night. On both occasions, I was alone in my caravan/trailer.

The first set of fifteen was received during a cold winter's night in May 2016, while the next six were during a warm spring November night in 2018.

The first fourteen are about God's expectations of the people of the world now and into the future. While the final seven are particularly about God and how we, God's people, need to interact with God.

Tears from God occurred several times around the receival of each Revelation. That mainly referred to the writing and releasing at the correct times - these twenty-one Revelations from God.

'We Need God' – Revelation 16

Until we can commit to, believe, and live this belief, we are nothing! We are limited to this world and all its imperfections, especially its 'holdbacks' and 'pushbacks'! The world is so very good at holding people back from everything that is their actual, highest destiny. Their ultimate self-worth, their ultimate possibilities, their ultimate realities – WITH GOD!

We are still of this world and for this world - until we take the leap. Until we truly believe and know, we must go beyond our natural, human, every day understood capacities.

To go beyond this world, to a higher existence, while still living in this world, we have no option other than to NEED GOD! Need God in its most real sense. Yes, NEED God.

This is much greater than needing a parent, a spouse, an education, a job, money, a career, or a friend, as examples. Much more significant than needing physical and emotional securities. Much higher than having all those expected and inherent, yet often withheld, human rights, social justices, and freedoms.

Once we accept the need for God and start developing our relationship with God, we progress towards God. We can initially become one with God while still living our lives on this earth. We then live a loving life with God and other people on the same journey. Our lives become more godlike. Those we mix with and live with should become a part of this Godness/goodness! We can help transform others once we know, appreciate, and attempt to live towards God's perfect ways, as well as we can with God being the number one priority in our lives.

The need is one of understanding and appreciating who God is, what God is for us individually and communally, and ultimately needing God to lead, guide, and be with us on all levels.

We all need to freely accept the reality of God, the awesomeness of the ultimate LOVING God, and the need to have God with us intrinsically and absolutely in our journey towards God throughout our lives. We need God! God needs us - out of love!

> We need God!
> God needs us - Out of love!
> That's Absolute True Love.

> Once we accept the need for God,
> And start developing our relationship with God,
> we progress towards God.
> We can become one with God
> while still living our lives on this earth…

'We need to be vulnerable to God' – Revelation 17

Imagine being somewhere surrounded by the most influential people in the world. People coming from various places, countries, companies, religions, parliaments, unions, etc. People we are expected to believe are the best possible in their particular lifestyles, faiths, beliefs, and occupations. How would you feel? How would you react?

Many of us would be overawed and would probably react strangely in the first instance. Some people would feel very much at home and engage quite quickly with members of this elite group. So much would depend on our self-confidence, experience and faith within such a group.

Let us now imagine the group was, in fact, GOD! Not people but the almighty from throughout history. The divine, one and only God!

Most people would figuratively or literally fall to the ground or something similar showing and expressing their total vulnerability to God and acknowledging the divine, supreme leader as an absolute lover of His creation.

This is how we must react and respond to our GOD! We must accept who we are and where we are on this divine continuum. *We must show absolute vulnerability to our most loving GOD. That is our love for GOD! A love where we don't overly question, put on trial, challenge, or judge GOD!*

However, various members of humanity will act quite differently from each other. Some won't believe it! Some will deny it and try and convince others to do the same. Some will think equals, human and divine, surround them. *Yet, this is so wrong and disrespects the absolutely loving creator of the universe.*

We must show our vulnerability to God always! Be prepared to 'bow' to our most loving God forever. Being vulnerable leads to our admission of human weakness, needing God's strength to be what God wants for and from us genuinely-being as perfect as we can be for God and God's creations.

Just ask God sincerely every day for stronger faith, guidance and forgiveness - always!

> This is how we must react and respond to our GOD!
>
> We must accept who we are and where we are on this human life and divine continuum.

> We must show absolute vulnerability to our most loving GOD.
>
> That is our love for GOD!
>
> A love where we don't question, put on trial, challenge or judge - God!

'We need to be asking for God's help continually, and God's assistance & support – ALWAYS. 'No egos' getting out of control – Just ask for help. Always.' - Revelation 18

We must accept that we are dependent on God for everything! Yes, we have Free Will and an informed conscience to decide, yet God is there for us on every occasion we have - for every day, hour, minute, and second of our existence.

We live on a knife's edge, where anything could go right or wrong at any time! We need God to guide and direct us accordingly.

We must allow God to 'help, assist, and support' us on our life's journey. There is no place in our existence to think and act as if we are the equal, near to identical, or dare it to be said, even better than God - because we certainly are not! If believed, then these thoughts are very evil for those concerned.

These beliefs will move us away from God, not moving God away from us. God is always there for us, no matter how bad our life circumstances, how evil we may have become, how unworthy we may be of God's Love. However, *once people believe what is possible with God, they will then freely be able to move away from evil and back to God/Goodness!*

The difference in comparison between God and us is unimaginable to us. There is no way humanity can understand divinity. We can only fully accept divinity once we are with God in Heaven. Divinity is hugely more than in our physical world. We can only know in-depth knowledge of the natural material. To properly appreciate divinity, we need to be in Heaven, no longer physical, but 'spiritual' and perfect.

There are various signs, Revelations, and inspiring messages, which point us in the right direction to have some idea of the magnitude and possibilities offered to us by God. And therefore, these signs, etc., are disclosing how we may do this. The divine and divinity are unimaginable to most of us. There is so much living, study, questioning God and prayer, etc. we must do before we can honestly relate better with GOD on higher levels. In the early stages, our openness to God is a great start. Being open and willing to give it a go, trying to hear and know God, are all parts of growing closer and developing our extra-special relationship with God.

As Revelation 18 states, 'No big heads'. How 'everyday' is that statement? You would imagine that almost everybody in the world would understand it. *We need God's guidance, directions, continual forgiveness, and laws (commandments and teachings/ beliefs).*

No-one is above God's laws, directions, and guidance. We are so far away from God in reality that we urgently need God's assistance throughout our lives. It is especially required when in trouble, ill or injured, moving away from God, losing the appreciation of God's place within our lives, having our faith challenged, etc.

Never give up on God or on the way that God can help us in any of our difficulties, problems, negativity in relationships, etc

We must accept that we are dependent on God for everything!

…God is there for us on every occasion we have –

for every day, hour, minute and second of our existence.

We need God to guide and direct us accordingly.

…We have to respond as God requires!

We are insignificant compared to God' – Revelation 19

The reality is that God is so superior to humans that we cannot appreciate this reality in any way what-so-ever as adults. As humans, we cannot get our appreciation of God anywhere near the Truth of God. The divine creator of the universe is beyond humanity's understanding. Yet, we must aim for strong faith and belief in God and God's ways of assisting His creations.

The better we grow in our spiritual skills, obedience, forgiveness, relationships, along with our faith and belief in God and all that is possible with God, etc. and with our fellow humans, the closer we will become to the divine God also.

We will experience a more peaceful and rewarding existence. It is because we move closer and closer to God in our beliefs and actions. The closer we get to God, the more of God's absolute love, we will be receiving from the Divine God.

We must acknowledge our insignificance to God. When we can accept this insignificance, we can also accept that we are constrained by our humanity when compared to God. We need to acknowledge this reality, respectively. Yet, there are and have been, billions of humans existing on our Earth for millennia.

So what does this insignificance mean for us?

We need God well beyond whatever we have imagined! We can float along as many people do. Or, we can admit our station in life and creation and legitimately turn to God for the essential support we need as humans.

One of the most significant aspects of our lives is to make this happen! To *accept our 'insignificance compared to God' and to then move forward with God's assistance, support, and guidance.*

When we accept that God is on our side and wants the best for all of us, many outstanding results are possible - for each of us!

God desires for all of us to be saved. To meet God 'face-to-face' in Heaven. We know this from various Revelations and inspired messages received by humanity over the millennia. God's love for each individual is so far beyond what we can imagine that we must allow this relationship to grow and prosper and become our everyday reality. *All this is out of our love for God and the openness to 'hear and believe' what God 'tells us' or directs us out of 'His' absolute love. Heaven awaits the faithful, forgiving, loving humans.*

God desires for all of us to be saved.

To meet God 'face-to-face' in Heaven.

God's love for each individual is so far beyond what we can imagine
that we must allow this relationship with God to grow and prosper and become our everyday reality.

> ... We need God well beyond whatever we had imagined!
>
> ... we can admit our station in life and legitimately turn to God
>
> for that essential support we need as humanity...

> When we accept that God is on our side and wants the best for all of us,
>
> many outstanding results will occur...

Humanity - 'God is So Superior and Divine – face up to it. Cut the egos back to being human – not divine!!! Believe it! Stop fighting it!' – Revelation 20

Today's world, in general, *but especially the western world, is moving away from God and institutional religions. Often there is a lack of appreciation of God and the beliefs by these people. Many people would say they are following God but not a religion.* It could certainly be the case. But what is best for each person in their relationship with God? It is found out individually by each person, plus through their religious/secular groups. It is also through their search for God and Goodness that it becomes known. Searching occurs throughout our lives as our relationship with God, and other people change and develop over time.

For a large proportion of the world's population, *there is a considerable misunderstanding these days of what a religion is, due to the very nature of faith. There is quite a large group within society who don't know what religious institutes are and how these operate. Nor the place of God in religions.* This lack of education or possible personal ignorance disadvantages the individual so much.

How many times would you have heard a parent say something like, "Oh, we don't want to pressurise our children to make decisions about religion and God until they are adults!" *It is giving children nothing for their search and on what to base their search. It sets them up for failure.* Unless the children's parents can explain and show their beliefs fully, over many years, then their children will be quite disadvantaged. *The other experience that affects the children is if their parents understand very little about God and religions-probably being the products of non-believing parents themselves.* These children would most likely not be attending a religious school for their education either.

If we accept from a fundamental viewpoint that *religion is some form of an institute of like-minded people trying to relate individually and communally to divinity, God, and God's people on Earth,* then these people are somewhere along the continuum to better understand and worship God. *Humanity must worship God - due to God being so superior and loving us all equally. God is without question the creator of the universe. God has demanded that we must see God as number One in all of creation, the world and existence.* This is not up for debate. Unfortunately, many people see themselves as the centre of the universe and act and think likewise. We must make this worshipping happen individually and collectively. As an example, the collective is the People of God. In Christianity, it is known as the Church.

Revelation #20 is not only considerably stating the obvious, but it is emphatic and clearly noted. There is no doubt at all that 'God is divinely superior' totally beyond anything we humans can imagine. Humanity must 'face up to it. Believe it! Stop fighting it!'

Too many people individually or communally are drifting along figuratively. Some are in the gentle wash of slow-moving water, up to others being caught in a tornado and thrown every which way.

> There is no doubt at all, that
> 'God is real & ultimately superior',
> that humankind must face up to it.
>
> Believe it!
>
> Stop fighting it!
>
> Revelations, Inspired Messages and Signs from God, should help us believe the reality of God.

A significant redirection back to God is now called for by God!

'Be meek & humble & real' – Revelation 21

These keywords are the opposite of how many people behave or believe how we should behave when we have an issue, belief or thought needing promulgation, etc. It is almost the opposite of what our society reacts to, no matter the politics of the country. Being loud and proud of your viewpoints are mostly encouraged. Quieter less domineering people often get lost amongst the chatter and quick 'movements' within our societies.

Being meek and humble and real is a significant challenge for many, if not most. Yet, this is what God has revealed for us to be like. *A rough, domineering, 'violent' leadership of any sort is not to be the case.*

Love is gentle, compassionate and forgiving. A leadership of true love is the ideal directed by God.

Initially, these words of Revelation 21 seem weak and powerless.

Yet some of the greatest leaders in history would be considered to have these attributes significantly. These would include the prophets over the millennia and *Jesus the Christ in particular. The prophet Jesus is also the incarnate God in Christianity. Mahomad also fits this concept in Islam due to his incarnation as well.* (Revelation #15)

The world needs more truthful religious, Godly narratives, and accurate, quality communication, between all people and religions. There are several religions whose teachings and beliefs don't always match the aim of God. *One example is any religion whose leaders or followers see violence as the answer to much of the world's or religion's place, are not meek, humble and real.*

They are not moving to a close relationship with God or humanity. Moses, Abraham and Noah are three of the major prophets for Judaism, Islam and Christianity and for all intents and purpose are genuinely, meek, humble and real. Gandhi, Martin Luther King and many others throughout history also have these extra-special traits in the preaching, teaching and lifelong examples of peace and love being shared with all. *These sorts of people, religious or not, being meek, humble and real, are setting the marker for everyone else to follow. Religious leaders, religious academics, followers of various faiths/religions, etc. are charged with developing these Revelations into the language and beliefs of each religion's followers.*

Only genuine, authentic, strong, holy people can 'be meek & humble & real' in its truest religious sense. God needs these types of people to assist with promulgating 'His' Revelations and Inspired Messages to our world.

> Only genuine, authentic, strong, holy people can 'be meek & humble & real' in its truest religious sense.

Too many people individually or communally are drifting along figuratively,

some in the gentle wash of slow moving water,

…others being caught in a tornado and thrown every which way.

God demands much better than this!

Being meek and humble and real is a major challenge for many.

No violence, no excessive ego, no fakeness!

This is what God has revealed for us to be like…

Renumbering Added Revelations

Various Revelations received in 2016 need to be renumbered at this stage of dissemination due to three being available now but were deliberately left off the original publications. This was so because it wasn't God's time for such announcements.

That time has changed and is to be highlighted now for Revelations #6, #13, #14, #15.

Revelation 6. Die for what is right.

Revelation 13. Cyberbullying – in all its forms, of all sorts, of all ages…

Revelation 14. Fear rules – often from the cyberworld – eliminate this.

Revelation 15. …Jesus and Mahomad is God

('is' on last line above is the actual word received and written as told by God – how can this be interpreted or explained? Both Jesus and Mahomad <u>are</u> the same God.

The question is why would God do this? Is it a code for something? Does someone else know the code and is waiting for its arrival? Etc.

Strange!)

'Die for what is right' – Revelation #6

This is the most challenging Revelation to understand and a way by which to live. The difficulties are mainly due to the limited engagement we have with death in our busy lives in a mostly secular and secure first world. Most people would react incredibly negatively to this proposition, even though it is now stated as a Revelation from God. *A new, major one, which will require considerable exploration, to truly appreciate its purpose and the actual necessity for our often misguided world.* Dying is often seen as the result of terrorism and war, crime, old age or accident. Sometimes due to an illness, particularly related to cancer, coronary issues, and deadly viruses, such as the coronavirus/Covid-19 in 2020 exemplify the incredible loss of human life to various viruses, bacteria and diseases, etc.

This Covid-19 pandemic has killed over 400 000 people so far and infected over 7 000 000 cases worldwide. Over

100 000 people died in the USA alone at the time of writing. There appears to be doubt about the accuracy of some of these numbers from various countries. These seem to be on the lower end of an accurate count. Some countries seem to be holding back much higher numbers. Either way, there is/was a catastrophic effect of Covid-19 worldwide. We need to be fully prepared for such events in the future too. Imagine if Ebola became a pandemic?!

Then we come to the unexpected, illegal, extremely evil deaths affecting many of the world, totally out of ignorance, false beliefs, and evil theology from various extreme religious leaders. Most striking of these is the religious Islamic Jihad. ISIS, a small minor Islamic force, is extremely violent and deadly. It is one of the aggressive, hateful groups of extremely evil terrorist forces these days, killing thousands of Muslims and others alike. These people are tortured and/or killed because they are not seen as following the extreme Sharia law. In ISIS minds, these people are evil and enemies of Allah/God.

There are two main religious jihads. Firstly, where people are striving to better themselves for God, they are fighting within themselves to be the best they can be for God and their families and communities. Then there is the violent defensive Jihad where the Muslim followers take up arms against anti-Sharia, Islamic foes. The classic example was the Crusades from approximately the 11th to 16th centuries ago across Europe and Middle-East. Many Crusades were for the reclamation of previous Christian lands from Muslims by Christian soldiers. It was taking back territory from the previous Islamic expansionism, including the Holy Land. Muslims believed that they were defending their Islamic religion and territories against the attacking Christians. (Brittania Encyclopedia)

Maybe this will help with gaining a deeper appreciation of the violence in Islam in Mahomad's time. Theologians and scriptural scholars (of Islam and Christianity, in particular) have now had a significant challenge placed before them. We all should pray for the experts to pray, research, study, share, discern, explore, etc. how this new

Revelation #6 (and #15 also) should apply in Islam and across other religions.

People generally want to live a long, fulfilled, rewarding, healthy life, as much as possible. So much in this world is pointing towards such a reality. Medicine and health, in general, have this as a primary aim. People often react with aghast at anyone mentioning dying young or old but not ill enough for a natural death.

It somehow seems that as humans, we seem to need to live as long as we possibly can, no matter our health, etc. But this is mostly wrong in the context of God's love for us. What about the quality of life?

Most people would enter into a serious discussion when this topic is introduced to most conversations. Because of our exceptional medical and health professionals keeping people alive well beyond our historically accepted 'expiry' date, people want the right to die when circumstances are most challenging and a life of pain, or solitude, or coma or the vegetive state, etc. are the only outcomes. Morphine helps people in significant difficulties with unrelenting pain from various illnesses, etc. Euthanasia is becoming a major issue and response to relentless, considerable pain, various debilitating diseases, quality of life, etc. in the western world.

To die for what is right requires considerable discussion and openness to various viewpoints. At birth, there will be a situation that arises whereby either the mother or the child may need to die in childbirth. A horrendous decision is necessary.

There will be times that the fabric of our society comes under major attack or threat from either external or internal local or worldly threats. It could include cyberwar, terrorism, war, extreme weather conditions, e.g. tornados, tsunamis, hurricanes/ cyclones, domestic violence, torture, contagious illnesses, suicide, life-destroying accidents, incarceration, severe viral diseases, e.g. coronavirus/Covit-19, Ebola, etc.

How we react to these, and many other issues, will dictate the outcome – good to bad. We may respond as individuals or communally. We may defend our spouses, children, colleagues, or self, etc. It all may end with us not surviving the attack, whatever it may be.

We must ask the question of all questions. What would it take for me to place my life on the line to save others or myself? Could I do it if the urgency arose?

If we place this in the context of our lives within our western world, we see that numerous people and groups are living this option every day of their lives. For example, police, military, paramedics, fire and rescue, to name but a few occupations, are giving of themselves for our safety and survival. Sometimes with their own lives, to protect us, the other members of our society, or others.

Everyone should imagine themselves in various hypothetical circumstances and try and gauge how we should react or prepare for such atrocities, accidents or illnesses, etc. What would it take for you to put your own life at risk to save yourself, family or others? What would you need to do before this resulted in preparation for your response?

It is quite amazing how people within our world will lay down their lives for others if the unavoidable circumstances arose. They will die for what is right when no other response or possibility is available, i.e. imagine the reaction we have already seen to world wars, particularly for our soldiers in WW1 and WW2, right up to today's ISIS and other terrorist wars impacting on thousands of people, most being innocent civilians. Many soldiers and others involved will refuse the hero tag, as they see their reaction/response as what they imagine anyone would do under the circumstances. Would you?

It must be remembered that even though life is sacred and extraordinary and that it is our human duty to value it uppermost and save it wherever and whenever possible, there may be times when we have to offer the ultimate sacrifice, risk our lives and die - for what is right, possibly, on a significant community scale.

'We Stand for God' is a beautiful quote and a powerful hymn!

If we live, we live to the Lord, and if we die, we die to the Lord; so then, whether we live or whether we die, we are the Lord's. (Romans 14:8)

There is no need to prolong life just for the sake of getting old artificially. However, this seems to be the case at this time in our history for many.

Do you have to wonder about preserving life no matter the reason? So that it can be done? More people are starting to see this as what it is – unnecessary, life-prolonging, and at times, something from which no-one will gain.

I often wonder why we do this, mainly when we know and believe that God is waiting for us to return to Heaven and become one with 'Him' again? Is this a sign that we don't believe in Heaven or God? Or maybe it's a matter of betting both ways – just in case it isn't the Truth?

It must be remembered, that even though
life is absolutely sacred and extremely special,
and that it is our human duty to value it uppermost and save it wherever and whenever possible,

**there may be times when we have to offer the ultimate sacrifice and die for what is right,
possibly on a major scale.**

Reader:

What would it take for me
to place my life on the line
to save others, or myself?

Could I do it if the urgency arose?

'Cyberbullying – in all its forms, of all sorts, of all ages...' – Revelation #13

'Welcome to the 21st century.' Not so actually from a cyberbullying viewpoint, unfortunately!

Now that cyberbullying is close at hand and affecting so many people simultaneously, it is or has been, time to solve this significant worldly problem. And what a world problem it is. This cyberbullying seems to be growing at an incredibly fast rate. It is now a part of so many people's actual daily lives – for the worse.

Fake news, fake information and scammers are forever proliferating! Key people are involved. Various political leaders, media entities, university lecturers and researchers, etc. seem to be engaged at multiple times to add a level of stress and the unfair challenging of differing views for anything different or slightly different to their particular liking. The PC (politically correct) world is proliferating. Yet we still must allow our populations to have freedom of speech, movement, beliefs, etc., even if these aren't seen as PC correct by various people. Yet stop all hate speech and violence.

Indeed, the level of unacknowledged bias is increasing considerably. While so-called political correctness is becoming or has already become, a dominating force in the world, the cyber world has its considerable share, yet this need not be so.

When the loud radical minority has the cyber ability and other media outlets to shut down genuine debate and different opinions, we are in serious trouble as a world of various differing and valuable cultures and religions.

All people are capable of being cyberbullied in so many ways. The number of trolls who comb the internet looking to 'smash' someone is considerable. They 'get off' on this hidden attack mode. Their dark cyber world often encourages this form of attack on innocents. *Innocence is lost by so many people being attacked: no justice, no consideration, no love at all being shown by these cyberworld attackers.* However, a number of these slanderous posts etc. are being taken to court and winning! *It seems that society is fighting back against such massive behemoths of social media, along with various academics, media personalities and organisations, etc.*

At this present time in history, several key countries are seriously looking into the options the cyberworld has of harm, slander, etc. *Slowly but surely, various countries and people are fighting back against the 'dark' world's harming of people everywhere.* These evil hackers, etc. seem to believe they have the power, *yet they hide in the cyberworld from those affected so considerably.* Massive court fines have been issued across the world to stop such practices, and so these should. Money talks to these monstrous social media organisations. Hefty penalties are necessary for balanced world order.

All these above challenges can close down genuine debate on controversial yet necessary topics, also on fundamental rights, particularly the right to free speech, religious freedoms and free movement.

This free movement became a serious issue this year as a result of the coronavirus/Covid-19. At the time of writing this book, millions of people have it worldwide, and hundreds of thousands of deaths have occurred. More will occur before any vaccine is developed, along with other health process es being discovered, etc.. Governments are mostly acting in the right way to defeat this virus. Borders domestic and international have been closed, various cruise liners have been refused berthing rights, the economies worldwide have seen major capital, investment and businesses fall considerably in value, and life is becoming more difficult for most people in the western world in particular. *There then becomes the knock-on effect for the third world countries, reliant on the western world for significant assistance, mainly economic and health-wise.*

When the loud radical minority has the cyber ability and other media outlets to shut down genuine debate

and differing opinions,

we are in serious trouble as a world of various different and valuable cultures and religions.

'Fear rules – often from the cyberworld – eliminate this…' – Revelation #14

These days there is a considerable lack of privacy, mainly due to the internet and social media. God needs His people to eradicate this 'disease'. *It is not God doing these evil things to people, but it is people freely choosing to do so to each other, even though all are aware that it is not in anyone's interest to be so hurtful to fellow human beings.* Some common areas of potential fear, which somehow impact on most people, are listed:

- There is an avalanche of information, news and personal views, often making it very difficult to separate fact from fiction – primarily due to fake news and fake information.
- There is constant surveillance, even in the home with many people not even aware of who is watching and listening and how and why.

- Is your laptop, television, tablet, smartphone, or your Google and Amazon home device, etc. keeping an eye on you even more than you are on it?
- There is an explosion of online purchases and electronic money transfers. How trustworthy are those who access and use your banking and financial information?
- How much faith do we place on what people say, show, do, engage with, or ignore us through the cyber world?
- All the internet searches we do, comments we make and people we engage with on social media, companies we buy from, videos and music we stream are recorded.
- Blogs, articles, personal and professional websites we write or comment on or share or follow.
- Videos we upload or download from YouTube, Vimeo, Facebook, etc. So many platforms are available.

- Internet calls we make whether video or audio - most telephone calls these days, are digitally based.
- Messages and txts we send or receive.
- Photographic images or video we make and share digitally.
- Clubs or agencies of which we are members and with which we interact.
- What security is enforced with personal information, accounts, bios and images?
- Etc.

So many 'terms and conditions' exist, which very few read, mostly because these are so long and often confusing. It seems that many organisations seem to pursue this method, that obviously favours them.

We often hear or read of people's troubles with these cyber formats. *The lack of privacy. The opportunities for abuse. The often-compelling thought to get out of social media groups before they get you. But often most people would let that go and react otherwise, not necessarily being too concerned.* These people engage on a day to day, hour to hour, minute to minute and more than ever second to the second occasion with the cyber world. Because it is seen as just so usual and every day, the underlying fear and genuine concern often become masked from people's realities.

However, *ultimately an underlying fear pervades the knowing and unknowing of each platform alike. Fear of what could be in store for the unwary or manipulated. Fear of being taken advantage of ripped off or abused. The more we become aware of the sustained and significant influence of the cybersphere's fearful impact on each of us, the higher our need to address these influences just to remain safe and in control of our lives (as much as this is even possible these days).*

These are just some of the cyber world issues. These are incredibly significant issues, which could become considerable and culturally substantial, even lifestyle or life-threatening if due care and attention aren't at the forefront of our lives and planning.

The world must seriously consider life options beyond the immediate and almost whole of life place the cyber-sphere plays in our lives. *The second and third worlds are thirsting for what the first world has* and in similar proportions, which is not possible, at this stage. *Could this be one of the most exceptional opportunities offered to them — to see how fortunate they are in being able not to add this to their massive list of difficulties?* (Even though it is also becoming their reality as it is forced through poverty, lack of power and selfish politics from various wealthy countries, companies and individuals.)

Taking the moral high ground while standing in the swamp doesn't appeal to too many people though. *The best we can do is to help all people from all worlds, those with and those without these cyberworld options, to see the huge benefits, as well and huge disadvantages, that the cyber world offers. To help all people make fully informed, rational decisions in their best interests.*

We must do everything within our power to care for ourselves and others who get caught up with the 'dark side' of the internet. *The evildoers of the cyberworld are many and need to be called out and taken out of their 'safe' environment and dealt with judicially and quickly.* Their harm can be irreparable and often lead to the death of innocent young people, in particular. Suicide becomes an option for many of these younger ones. But anyone can be so affected.

We genuinely need to be aware of the lack of privacy, the abusers, the rip-off merchants, the thieves of data and identity, the fake news and information providers and all the forms of evil lurking and found in the cyber world.

These negatives cause so much angst and fear amongst the populations. Once we are aware, we then need to fight these with all the resources at our disposal – *the law and law enforcement are critical.*

We should also fight this fear ethically through all our institutions, especially the religious, legal, educational and social justice ones.

The more we become aware of the sustained and significant influence of the cybersphere's fearful influence on each of us,

the greater our need is to seriously address these influences just to remain safe and in control of our lives…

(Edited Extract from *Where's God? Revelations Today*, 2018, by Bryan Foster, p107-9)

CONCLUSION

God's People, all of us who have been born along with those yet to come, are at a very special junction in the history of humankind. These People are all the ones who are, will be, or have already lived their lives on Earth (and elsewhere if that is at all possible?) Remember that God can do anything and that we can't challenge God! We live on totally different planes of existence. God's presence is divinely spiritual and fully creative, while our's is primarily physical, but with some spirituality and a touch of creativity. God comes to our plane deliberately to inform, advise and teach what is required for that special relationship with God. God is absolute Love who loves each human absolutely equally and desires for us to choose to exist in Heaven with God at our death.

The juncture to which we are now placed has the two largest religions, Christianity and Islam, being told that one of their significant beliefs is shared across both these religions. That God became Incarnate in both faiths, i.e. God became human at two specific times in history, that we are now aware of - in the first century was Jesus and sixth/seventh century was Mahomad. God lived totally as a human, as Jesus Christ and Mahomad, amongst His earthly creation and eventually went back as God in Heaven.

To claim that Jesus, God, Mahomad, Allah (+ Yahweh for the Jews and Brahman for the Hindus) are all the same God and Incarnate human God for Christianity and Islam, is a massive claim. Yet it was a Revelation from God to humanity through this book's author, in one instance, and possibly in other people's experiences worldwide? Time will tell. Time will also determine if other religions also have an Incarnate God experience for them, e.g. Hinduism, with all its Gods being manifestations of the one God, Brahman.

Maturity of the reader, theologian, scriptural scholar, priest/minister, etc. needs to be a very high priority here. Fundamentalists, with respect, from any of these religions, could take an extreme approach to deal with this newfound information about Jesus and Mahomad. The religions that teach that there are no more prophets since the last in their various scriptures are probably too fundamentalist at this stage to truly appreciate and learn from God. Yes, God's ways are unknown, yet we do know that God can do anything, anytime, anywhere, always.

There can not be any violence resulting from this new teaching! It is the author's understanding that the time is now right according to God for this belief to be pronounced as legitimate. Up until now, the world wasn't considered ready. God has advised that now is the time in history and that this belief is genuine and necessary to understand and be taught.

The author of this book is one of the links to people within each of the legitimate religions mentioned. (Other faiths not mentioned may also like to be involved, whether they have a present-day prophet or not.)

God has informed the author through Revelations from God to him, prayer, inspired messages and Tears from God that he was genuinely an authentic spiritual person chosen by

God for this first endeavour of making this belief public through this new book's publication.

The definitive moments where the author received the 21 Revelations from God occurred in the early morning when he was awoken from sleeping in his caravan/trailer at the foot of Mt Warning, Australia. Firstly at the Murwillumbah Showgrounds in town in May, 2016, and next at the Mt Warning Rainforest Park camping grounds on the drive up to the walkers' starting point in November, 2018.

The following step in the process of informing an interested world as to what we imagine is the meaning of the Revelation, how we are to appreciate it and to what it may lead comes next.

The 'ball' (this book) is now being passed to the religious specialists for each authentic religion wanting an involvement with this process: i.e. religious leaders, theologians, and authoritative scholars, etc. to add the necessary depth and understanding of its meaning and its place in the mainline religious world. To instruct and encourage the followers of each religion and denomination how this new-found knowledge will be incredibly freeing for those open-minded enough to accept where this now takes us.

This Book Five in the *'GOD Today' Series* brings us to the beginning of an exciting whole new world through which we all may exist! To accept freely, these new Revelations can only help us all to become closer to God while on this earth and eventually, one with God entirely in Heaven.

Nothing in these new just released beliefs takes anything of substance away from any religion. It does the opposite, i.e. it adds considerably to each religion. This belief is incredibly freeing for the followers of both faiths, and from other religions for whom this will challenge or carry them to a different but necessary level.

There is a definite advantage for those who can accept it. Just as we discussed in the 'one God only' belief, starting in the first book of this series, we need to be open to new beliefs from God – when God wishes these shared with our world.

Where has this Series taken us so far?

We have been given 21 Revelations plus numerous inspired messages from God through the Revelations and messages sent to the author. One of these has challenged us to accept that one God is the only God for all religions, for all times, for all cultures, etc. Each Revelation has now been explained, either in this Book 5 or one of the earlier publications. We have seen photographic images in Books 2 and 4 which may have been quite challenging, (especially Book 4), yet hopefully challenged us to accept that the Revelations and Inspired Messages looked at throughout the Series, are relevant and highly necessary in today's world.

The most challenging Revelation for most people will be #15, I believe, due to its significant theological development. God/Allah/Brahman/Yahweh are all the One and only God. Jesus and Mahomad are God Incarnate, i.e. God becoming fully human.

The author is amazed at how creative God is, especially in letting those who have been invited to assist in the dissemination of new Truths go. So much of the spectacular photobook, Book 4, really shows God's creativity in action for us today. Of course, this isn't anything magical from God – just the norm!!! To gain highly from this series, reading Book 4 would be considered quite central and necessary, especially due to its unique and stunning photographic images, challenging us from God.

It is the most spectacular way of sharing God's Revelations and Inspired Messages. God's use of the sun provided photographic arrows, flares, rays and double rainbows. One striking example was rays emanating out of a small cloud sitting atop of Mt Warning certainly make a unique point. This image is the cover photo of Book 2. The sun arrows passing 'closely' over, through or across the author or the author's books in the photographs taken at various destinations in Australia and Canada, are quite challenging, yet true events.

The *'GOD Today' Series* has brought some serious challenges to the reader, yet nothing more than should be the case, as it is God who is guiding the whole process. 'He' hopes that the reader will also be affected as deeply as the author has. The author has used God's guidelines to assist with the dissemination of the Revelations and Inspired Messages. Keeping the descriptions and explanation in everyday language wherever possible, hopefully, inspires many to 'give it a go' and see with what God is challenging us.

To assist readers at various faith levels, or those who have read some but not all of this *Series'* previous books, are the detailed appendices, which immediately follow the conclusion of this Book 5. These appendices, along with several earlier book edited extractions, add much of the necessary background throughout this book. Key placements of various topics covered across the *Series*, also aid a better understanding and appreciation of our most loving God and God's People. Relevant details, strategically placed throughout, hopefully, help make these books easier to read, understand and accept for what they are – God's Revelations and Inspired Messages to our world today.

> The historic, religious paradigm, in which we are now placed, has the two largest religions,
>
> Christianity and Islam,
>
> being told that one of Christianity's major beliefs is shared across both these religions.
>
> That God became Incarnate in both religions
>
> i.e. God became fully human at two specific times in history, that we are now aware of,
>
> in the first century, Jesus, and sixth/seventh centuries, Mahomad.

God lived totally as
a human,

as Jesus Christ and
Mahomad,

amongst 'His'
earthly creation and
eventually went
back as God in
Heaven.

Bryan Foster

Essential Background

Appendix 1

What are Revelations and Inspired Messages from God?

This book refers to Revelations as being those inspired messages coming directly from God through a unique encounter with God and the person receiving these. However, there should also be some form of 'proof' of this reality, such as Tears from God and other justification points (explained shortly) before it is entirely accepted and shared as the Truth. Inspired messages are those thoughts and points received through prayerful experiences or other people, nature or events -from wherever God is inspiring us. However, a process of discernment is needed to clarify the authenticity of these and is different from ordinary thoughts and feelings.

The concept of 'Revelations' in this book are also referred to as 'Special or Direct Revelations' in various religious circles in society. God specifically directs these Revelations to individuals or groups. What is referred to as 'inspired messages' in this publication may, at times, be referred to as 'General Revelations' in other religious publications and discussions? These are from God to anyone in general, being received through such means as nature, ethical appreciations and cognitive reasoning. (GCSE, BBC) Christianity believes that Jesus is the ultimate example of the fullness of Revelation observed on this earth by humanity. (Oxford Scholarship, 2018) The different religions have various appreciations of the relevance of Revelations historically and today. All genuine religions believe that God reveals Godself to this world through various forms, especially through people, their beliefs and morality, and through the natural world.

The terms 'Revelation' and 'inspired messages' are used as points of clarity. Naming every message with which God inspires humanity with the word 'Revelation' may become confusing as there are different levels of Revelation. 'Revelation' is used when there is direct contact of God with specific people, while 'inspired messages' are for those revelations discerned by people as emanating from God. How both of these occur is explained.

This book is primarily about explaining the various Revelations I received directly from God in 1982, 2016 and 2018, along with the inspired messages received from God and discerned over more than thirty-five years. There is an inherent, authentic sense of the Truth being shared.

The literary style is one of stating the Revelations and inspired messages received or discerned from God accurately without diminishing the emphasis of each through diplomatic, political or politically correct forms.

The key Revelations and inspired messages will be stated clearly and without a softening or hardening to appease certain groups who may not fully or partially agree with each statement. Each Revelation and inspired message will be explained in enough detail so that the point is made succinctly and clearly.

There is a real emphasis on Keeping it Simple for God's People. Too often religious preachers, teachers and theologians emphasise too much detail beyond the clarity of the message. People then get lost in all the detail, and the point from God is missed. This book aims to keep the messages simple yet explained with enough detail for a proper understanding to be gained.

This book is not an apologetic work. It is not teaching or preaching a set of one religion's doctrines over another religion's. It is not standing up and fighting for any particular religion or religious leader or any specific belief or patterns of faith from any particular religion.

It is a book of the Truth about and basically from the forever One and Only God of existence.

All genuine religions are equal and have an essential role from God for each of their followers. The belief in only one God is most liberating and beneficial for appreciating and following God.

This truth is the Truth of God for today's global and interconnected world. The following section explains why I make this claim.

It has been quite a journey to get to this point. It began in 1982 when receiving the Tears from God and physical warmth flowing from head to foot received as part of the gift of healing from Sister Ann at a secondary school's Commitment Day. Over the interim period from 1982 until now so much has been discerned as being God's inspired messages. This discernment process is explained.

After receiving God's Revelation in 2016, explained in various ways and sections throughout the book, the initial reaction was one of doubt - even though there were many Tears from God on many occasions privately and with my wife, Karen, to show its authenticity and genuineness.

When it came to the crunch to decide what would be highlighted in the first book in this *'GOD Today' Series, 1God.world: One God for All*, I wasn't able to run with all the Revelations. I was only able to highlight the 'One God only – One God' Revelation and some subsequent discerned inspired messages from God and stories of experiencing God throughout my life. A real doubting Thomas scenario occurred. In hindsight, I now believe this was all part of God's plan. God initially wanted me to highlight the One God Only Revelation, along with the messages and stories contained in that edition.

This approach used for the first book in this *'GOD Today' Series* opened up the opportunities for me to grow into the other Revelations this past couple of years and to discern a better appreciation of each. To also gain the courage to be able to go out into the world and state these with authority. It wasn't to be just a matter of listing these but to believe strongly in each one and to explain each one in detail. God wanted these Revelations to become part of the world's meaningful and fully understood lexicon.

We all need to appreciate these Revelations and what these mean so that we can each make the Revelations an integral part of our lives.

Hence, this second book is written with a higher level of understanding and appreciation than the previous edition. It includes so much more on both the Revelations from 1982 and 2016 and the original and subsequent inspired messages from God.

(Edited Extract from *Where's God? Revelations Today*, 2018, by Bryan Foster, p35-38)

Appendix 2
Mt Warning – Word of God Revelation – the Story

In 2016 God 'came down' from the mountain. This most majestic Australian 'mountain' in the Northern Rivers, NSW, and offered forth a most remarkable experience of God for the author. Having just spent three days touring around Mt Warning, reflecting on it, photographing and videoing it and staying in a caravan/trailer park on its plain, all was to culminate in a nighttime oneness with God event. This Revelation moment is indelibly etched on my whole being.

I had the most remarkable opportunity to experience God's Word firsthand, literally. I had taken leave to recuperate from illness and stayed for a few days in a caravan in my wife's original hometown. The campsite I chose significantly had a view of Mt Warning in the background. A 'mountain' I had viewed thousands of times over the years, particularly since I was 18 and had met my future wife and her local farming family. Mt Warning is an imposing 'mountain' feature in the far north of New South Wales, Australia. I say mountain, in reality, it isn't in any comparative height-sense like the mountains of Europe/Asia or the Americas. For the oldest continent, Australia, it is quite imposing. Being a volcanic core, it stands out literally within the caldera features of a vast ancient volcano. The shape is very appealing and attractive. Its centrality within the region causes it to be a feature admired from all directions.

Over three days, I drove the 72km around its base and up to the walkers' departure point (on bitumen and gravel roads). Around sugar cane farms and through national parks and small villages, I videoed and photographed it from all possible directions, sat and reflected with it, observed it, drove and walked to crucial observation points, visited its base, and became very familiar with it. You could almost say, I became one with it.

On the third day, I was awoken at night. I was very aware of my breathing and of breathing cold, fresh, clean air. I just lay there breathing deeply in through the nose, holding each breath for a couple of seconds and slowly blowing it out through the mouth. There was a real sense of presence. I started to realise it was quite a cold night and that I was lying at the foot of Mt Warning, relatively. I began to get this powerful awareness that I was one with the mountain. The mountain and I had grown together significantly these past three days, and now we were at a climax. The Truth would become apparent.

I then started to get a message to write down what I was about to receive. And to be very accurate.

I soon began to realise that, just as in ancient times, the mountain was a conduit to God. Prophets from many religions had climbed mountains to be closer to God and to receive God's message for that time and place in history and often for subsequent eras. I was not to climb the mountain tonight. (Or ever again due to an injury.) But I was to climb it figuratively.

Or was it a case of God coming down from the mountain?

Remarkably, what followed blew me away! Without thinking about what I was to write, I found myself writing down a list of instructions, teachings, 'refreshers'. Was it truly from God? It sure felt like it. But how could I tell? I was told within my mind not to overthink this; to go with the flow - that it was all legitimate and would become apparent as the night went on. The challenge for me was that since my 25th birthday religious experience (See 25th birthday story in Appendix 5, p.292ff), tears were a sign for me of God's presence, the greater the tears, the greater the divine presence. (See 'Tears from God')

Yet, there were no tears tonight. But there was ecstasy and a realisation of what was happening. A font of wisdom was unfolding, and I was so, fortunately, a part of it. The list was completed. An explanation from me of what had occurred was recorded after the list. (See 'Revelation

Notes' after the 'God's 12 Revelations' section.) And a perfect sleep followed.

The next morning was a Sunday, and I attended the Catholic sacrament/ritual of the Eucharist in the church in which Karen and I were married forty years ago this year! The mass was by coincidence a First Communion Mass for the local Catholic school. During the Mass, I asked God if what happened last night was real – what followed was an outpouring of tears. The answer was an emphatic, "Yes!"

> I then started to get a message to write down what I was about to receive…
>
> I soon began to realise that, just as in ancient times, the mountain was a conduit to God.

(Edited Extract from *Where's God? Revelations Today*, 2018, by Bryan Foster, p58-60)

Appendix 3

Inspired Messages - Afternoon of 28 May, 2016

That same Saturday, but in the afternoon, I received some inspired words, which are the ones following. In hindsight, these were an actual precursor for what was to be experienced that night.

God sits with permanent tears in his eyes.

Not the warrior image.

But the loving, caring, for all others...

The body truly is the Temple of God.

> Purify it
>
> Don't harm, poison it... illicit drugs, smoking...

(See explanations in *Where's God? Revelations Today*, 2018, Great Development Publishers, p115-127)

Appendix 4

Author's Autobiographical Life Events' Overview Leading to the 'GOD Today' Series. Ages 10 to 62.

Age

10-16 Sports' success – surf lifesaving nippers, basketball, rugby league, athletics, cricket and swimming. Learning to accept success. Included state champion wins at nippers, basketball Qld Vice-Captain (U16) in Sydney at national titles…

16 Treated poorly by a senior secondary school leader and middle manager due to my parents' choice for me not to play rugby league (football) in the firsts in year 11 – justice was missing. Winning College Open Athletics as a sixteen-year-old in yr 11 – justice felt here after a terrible year from the treatment from specific staff and students.

16-17 Treatment from the senior secondary school leader – also vetoed me from school leadership positions in year twelve. Justice denied the previous year. I earned a prefecture in my senior year despite his veto. It was announced in August on the rugby league grand final football school assembly morning, of our grand-final day. I was permitted by parents to play due to the suffering experienced through year 11.

17 Changing from BSc to Dip of Teaching. Partially due to an end of year address from a past student about the number ratio of girls to boys at McAuley Teachers College, Brisbane? A new venue for males training as teachers.

Plus wonderful mentoring/inspiration from years 11 and 12 teachers: Max Williams (Biology), Brian Dunlea (English and Religious Education) and Peter O'Brien (Mathematics A and B)

21 Commenced the newly introduced Diploma of Religious Education (DipRE) through the new Institute of Faith Ed at Catholic Education Brisbane. Choice of RE mainly seen as the future of Catholic schools – a career decision more than religious at this stage in my life. Little was I to know the incredible advancements I was to make towards God over the following decades. Over

the coming years, my love for teaching religion continued to grow. Hence my choice of academic courses needed specialised in religious studies to gain a BEd, a Grad.Dip.R.E. and an MEd (RE)

Marriage to Karen, my greatest supporter and the love of my life, whom I met at McAuley Teachers College. Her original plan was to go to ANU to be a teacher-librarian. Through a couple of compelling reasons, Karen chose not to go after all, but to go to McAuley. We met in Karen's first year and my second of three years. Married three years later. Purchased our first home at Macgregor, in the southside of Brisbane.

24 Moved from primary to junior secondary/high teaching, at Seton College, Brisbane – a unique, specialist school for average students plus those with issues in a ratio of 50/50. There were about 100 applications. The principal floored me when she explained that mine kept standing out when all were laid on the floor and without her reading any. I was then selected. This position lasted from January to May. Most difficult teaching ever. No specialised

teacher training for students with issues plus education at a higher level – went from yr 6 to years 8-10.

24 First baby girl daughter, Leigh-Maree.

25th birthday. Seton's 'Commitment to God Day'. My last day in secondary before moving to the country as a primary/elementary school principal at Tara. At Seton College, *I was prayed over by charismatic principal Sr Ann – and experienced the warm flow of God from head to toe plus the Tears of God for the first time. Any doubts about God disappeared then too.*

25-6 Tara, country Queensland out from Dalby on the Darling Downs. Both the new principal (myself) and new parish priest (PP) due to previous resignations amidst school and parish turmoil. A challenging time for both new leaders. I worked very closely with PP over the period. Successfully gained approval for the school to get special funding as part of the federal government's country schools' hardship plan – PCAP (Priority Country Area Program). I taught composite classes in a 2.5 teacher school: 1-4 then 5 - enrolment about 40. Karen replaced me on my one day a week principal release.

26 Second baby. A son, Andrew.

27-8 Goondiwindi. I was the first lay principal following the Sisters of Mercy departure. However, a religious sister was APRE and my release teacher. We were promised the sisters' house on the school block as a principal's house – this never eventuated and we, therefore, needed to buy our second home, this time in Goondiwindi. Eventually sold our Brisbane house during the time here, thinking we'd never be going back to Brisbane. Gave 'longest farewell speech in history', thinking I needed to get everything out there – learnt a valuable lesson – keep it simple (KiS) and keep it short (KiS)! i.e. KiSKiS.

Applied for Brisbane school jobs. Successful with Corpus Christi College (CCC), a girls' secondary school, (now renamed Mary McKillop College after Australia's first saint.) They said as long as I was sports' master for the two competitions they were in - state secondary girls and Catholic girls competitions. The challenge was accepted.

Immediately after accepting this, I was offered the principalship of the largest Catholic primary school in Toowoomba. Declined due to previous acceptance in CCC Brisbane – this experience strengthened my values of loyalty and giving one's word.

29-31 Returned to Brisbane to CCC as sports' master and teacher of newly created senior subject Study of Religion in its trial stage for BSSSS. Also taught PE, RE and basketball. I was the swimming and athletics senior coach.

30 World trip with my Dad. Supporting him with his hernia condition. Acting as support at Chicago World Mining Congress + in Saudi Arabia. Also visited east coast USA from Florida to NY, London, Bahrain, and Singapore. Special time with Dad. Experienced two Muslim countries firsthand – Saudi Arabia and Bahrain – had a major impact on me, especially their prayer regimes. Strong religious commitment.

31-2 Returned to Gold Coast. We built our house at Helensvale. I worked for two years at Marymount College at Burleigh and prepared students and staff for an introduction to the Study of Religion. The introduction occurred as I left for the next year.

33-4 Aquinas College. Year 11 Coordinator in further developed school from what was my previous boys' college. Aquinas went co-educational after the closure of the girls' Star of the Sea School in Southport. A significant challenge for the older former Aquinas' staff with the mixing of boys and girls.

35-6 Aquinas Acting APRE (Assistant Principal for Religious Education).

36-52 Marketing Manager (MM) – new role introduced. It was continued until age 52. Learnt on the spot - some assistance from, and to, newly created Communications Coordinator at my employer, Brisbane Catholic Education.

37-43 Aquinas' Years 11 and 12 Coordinator rotating each year with the same cohort over the two years + Marketing Manager

38 Birth of our third child, Jacqueline

41 Acting Assistant Principal Administration (Discipline and PC) 6 month + MM + teaching

42 Acting APA 6 months + MM + teaching

43 Acting APRE/REC 6 months + MM + teaching

44-52 APRE f/t + Marketing Manager + teaching

50 Term 4, three weeks of LSL at Lamb Island. Planned to start a reflections book but no inspiration, even with being surrounded by water and nature?! However, I started my marketing schools' book. In hindsight, I see this as a release from MM and passing on information gained in the role. Commenced a website, SMA (School Marketing Australia) and blogs to promote upcoming books, articles etc.

50-54 Wrote and released five marketing books – three editions for schools and two publications for churches. Latest in 2011 being *School Marketing Manual for the Digital Age (3rd ed)* and *Church Marketing Manual for the Digital Age (2nd ed)*

51 Changed roles. Moved to Brisbane Catholic Education to be an 'Education Officer Evangelisation and Spiritual Formation' f/t in Jill Goudie's team.

Major lower back slipped discs after World Youth Day activity at Roma Street Parklands. Homebound for three months. The injury resulted from 3-4 hours per day driving to and from Brisbane. I became overweight and unfit. I returned to Aquinas term four as an APA.

I started a company, School Marketing Australia. Unfortunately, I never got around to doing this marketing with the company - Health issues.

52 Final year as APRE. I had by necessity to retire from the position at the end of the year as the back was not improving with all the stress and

long hours of the APRE + MM position. Needed sustained recuperation time.

The birth of our first grandson, Kyan

53-60 Returned to f/t classroom teaching. The last 18 months was only years 8-10 by choice. The other forty years of education were mostly teaching SOR (30 years) for years 11 and 12, along with Religious Education and Religion and Ethics to senior levels. Fourteen years on the Study of Religion, Board of the Senior School Secondary Studies Panel, for Gold Coast and South Brisbane.

54 Changed company name to Great Developments Pty Ltd. Business name to Great Developments Publishers. Changed to publishing and marketing Karen's and my books, videos and photographs. Books are written by myself, with editorial and photographic assistance from Karen. Images also from son Andrew at Austographer.com. He now lives in BC Canada.

Birth of second grandson, Cruze.

56 Golden Staph illness fifteen nights in the local hospital.

58 Heart attack, plus stent placed in the heart.

59 Leg injuries. Long-time healing. Anxiety developed for most of the year.

Revelations from God at Murwillumbah, on the plains of Mt Warning on 29 May 2016. Writing and publishing book *1God.world: One God for All* – released November 25, 2016, on Karen and my 38th wedding anniversary.

I created a *1God.world* website. (Now named the *'GOD Today' Series*.)

60 Retired from f/t teaching in July. Chronically Stressed out + anxiety levels were very high. The only solution understood at the time was retirement - getting away from the f/t teaching problem. The problem is across all schools and mostly associated with newly expected subjects' assessment drafts marking, plus various time-consuming administrative requirements. There were way too many hours in addition to real, actual teaching. Offered to teach as a casual relief.

Eventually, I found out at the end of the year of other health issues relating to stress and retirement.

Forty-two years of teaching in Catholic Schools was celebrated.

Wrote next book in the *'GOD Today' Series - Mt Warning God's Revelations: Photobook Companion to '1God.world'*

61 Son Andrew and his wife Shannon in Canada had their first child, a beautiful little girl named Felicity – our first granddaughter and third grandchild.

Wrote and published the next two books in the *'GOD Today' Series – Where's God? Revelations Today* (October) and *Where's God? Revelations Today Photobook Companion: GOD Signs* (Nov 25)

Created author's websites:

https://www.BryanFosterAuthor.com

https://www.GodTodaySeries.com

https://www.facebook.com/groups/389602698051426/

Developed the *1God.world* website into the *'GOD Today' Series* website. This new website version is developing some pages for each original publication, blogs, etc., from 2016-21.

62 Wrote an article on the final two Revelations from the first Revelation night (2016), yet to be named or announced. An announcement video was made for these two. Both are embargoed for future release this year 2020. The title has now been finalised – *Jesus & Mahamod are GOD*. This is Book 5 now. Book 6 or 7 will be *Love is the Meaning of Life: GOD'S Love*.

62 Retired from teaching totally – 42 years of teaching religion in both primary/elementary and secondary schools. Birth of our second granddaughter, Isabella, to Andrew and Shannon in Canada.

I am now a part-time author and publisher of non-fiction books, videos and photographs.

63 Commenced a new website to concentrate on Book 5's themes, particularly the Incarnation

theme of both Jesus and Mahomad being God: *JesusandMahomadareGod.com*

Published and released mid-year *Jesus and Mahomad are God*. Aiming for *Love is the Meaning of Life: God's Love* by year's end. Hopefully, the second edition of *Love is the Meaning of Life* which is not a part of the *'God Today' Series*, as is the case for all the other mentioned books in this *Series*. It is for readers who are challenged too much by the God influence but have a need and desire to work through this.

> I am now a part-time author and publisher of non-fiction books, videos and photographs.

Appendix 5

Where it all began – Author's 25th Birthday

The day doubt disappeared, and my faith journey went to an unimagined higher level. On this day, I gained a whole new perspective of God and God's part in my life. Tears from God's love were experienced for the first time. The doubt about the reality of God disappeared. 'Let Go and Let God' became an actual spiritual reality of a profound order.

The stars all seemed to have aligned. It was my 25th birthday. As well as the school's uniquely offered, annual 'Commitment Day'. It was also my last day at this school. At the end of the day, I left this school for my first country school principalship – which began on the Monday after leaving Brisbane.

It started with birthday excitement but the last day of school sadness and ended in tears of absolute joy and oneness with God.

This school was unique in its philosophy and enrolment policy. One key difference to most schools was its strong association with the charismatic Catholic movement. This was especially manifested in the annual 'Commitment Day' to God. Various staff had special gifts from God, which they actively used within the charismatic movement, but are not limited to this movement. Many people have these multiple gifts from God but often aren't aware of such gifts. The other common one is Speaking in Tongues, which I have witnessed on many occasions. On this day, the seven teachers with the charismatic gift of healing were engaged for much of the time healing students and teachers alike. This healing encompasses any weaknesses we have, e.g. physical, emotional or social.

On this day the students and staff of this junior secondary Brisbane Catholic school began the day with a special Mass celebrated by a charismatic priest from Melbourne. The mass was followed by invitation to students and staff to commit to God sometime throughout the day. There was no compulsion, though. The students could roam the school freely throughout the day with the only prerequisite being no noise near the church. Staff supervised.

The staff of fourteen had seven charismatic teachers who had the spiritual gift of healing. One of these, the principal, was a sister in a religious order. Throughout the day there were a number of these charismatic teachers, plus the priest, present at various positions within the church. Students could choose who they would like to pray with when offering their commitment to God. Most stations would have many students continue with the staff member.

I sat with a particular student during the mass. This student was in a few of my classes. It took about an hour after mass concluded for this student to ask me to accompany her to pray with the principal and her present group of students. It was quite an event to go through the process to get there, due to various circumstances. However, once there, we were invited by the principal to move to the front of her group of eighteen to twenty students. Sister asked this student if she would like us to pray for her. She then asked me if I'd like to place my hand on the student's shoulder and pray. I agreed and prayed for her from very deep within my heart and soul - no speaking in tongues, just everyday English.

This belief in prayer causing healing, however, had caused me significant challenges that morning. I was tearing myself apart inside through the doubt that enveloped me about the whole healing circumstances that had been occurring in the church that past hour. Not being a charismatic person myself and having significant doubts about the entire healing process through a person being prayed over action, caused me major concerns. Much of this doubt was based on the television evangelists we would see on Sunday morning television back in the 1970s and 1980s where people were miraculously 'healed' in large numbers before our very eyes as if this was the norm. There was truth to many of these healings, yet there was always so much doubt, as well. It was remembering that many of these tele-evangelists eventually admitted to fraud or other inappropriate behaviours. I had also witnessed charismatics healing at a local Brisbane parish while eighteen years of age and at teachers' college. This had impressed me enough to want to consider it more. The tele-evangelists over the previous years up until this Commitment Day made belief in this healing process very difficult indeed.

So, as I walked this young lady to Sister, I was in incredible anguish internally. I was fighting against the possibility of something incredible. Each group had people who were crying or sniffling, and all were arm in arm with each other. It seemed to be too much for this doubter. Once I was asked by Sister to pray for the young lady, I instantly decided to 'Let Go and Let God'. This freeing moment was something quite unbelievable in itself. The confusion and doubt turned to belief and love. Sister then placed her hands on the girl's head and prayed. At that moment, the student broke down and tears freely flowed. I was now also tear-filled.

Next Sister asked if I'd like her to pray over me. What followed was life-changing. As she placed her hands on my head and prayed, there was this incredible feeling of heat flow from my head downwards to my feet. I then broke down and cried tears of absolute love for God and those around me. This is the moment in time that all my confusion, doubts and challenges about God disappeared.

Later that afternoon, I asked Sister what had happened, and she explained that it was God who came into me and that my old self was 'washed away' (downwards) and that I was 'filled up' with the new me.

I have remained so faith-filled and full of God's oneness and awe ever since – that is 36 years. My faith has never wavered since that day; even when some very challenging issues have confronted me. God was with me through each of these.

That was the day I truly learned that tears in specific instances are a sign from God - that God is truly present at that particular moment.

I am often asked if a similar experience of how God came to me, along with the Tears from God, will happen to others, to my students, their families and friends, my colleagues, etc. I genuinely believe that it could if the opportunity availed itself. We need to accept God's offer, whenever and wherever made. We may need to search out the possibilities. We may not expect it when it does happen. I believe the secret is always to be open to receiving God in both expected and unexpected ways. God loves us beyond our imagining and wants the best for each of us. We must not be blinded to God by all the distractions of this world. We need to be prepared for God to come in whatever way God chooses. It may not be what we expect, though.

We need to clear our minds and hearts to the beauty, purity and awesomeness that is God. We need stillness, openness and desire to accept whatever God offers, whenever God provides it.

The notion in much of the western world today is that we don't need God. It is either because we have so much or because we are blinded by so much - which is an absolute fallacy.

We need God as much today if not more as in any time and at any place in history have needed God.

It is the first significant time in history that the belief in God and acceptance of God being with us on this earth is diminishing. It is a time of absolute urgency requiring a major cultural shift towards God and God's people here today.

…there was this incredible feeling of heat flow from my head downwards to my feet.

I then broke down and cried Tears from God - of absolute love for God and those around me.

This is the moment in time that all my confusion, doubts and challenges about God disappeared.

(Edited Extract from *Where's God? Revelations Today*, 2018, by Bryan Foster, p131-135)

Appendix 6
'1God.world: One God for ALL'
(Book 1 in 'GOD Today' Series)

CONTENTS

Introduction

Author

PART 1
ONE GOD ONLY

Introduction to Part 1

KIS God – Keep It Simple

Why Believe in God?

God Loves You

1 God Only. For All.

1 God. 1 Name.

No One Religion

The 1 God Belief - Strengthens Personal Religious Belief

What the major world religions of Christianity, Islam, Hinduism and Judaism say about there being 1 God
    Religious Scripture
    Commentators' Views

PART 2
DISCOVERING GOD

Introduction to Part 2

Author's Story of Discovering God (Stories included)

PART 3
GOD'S MESSAGES FOR TODAY'S WORLD

Introduction to Part 3

Tears from God

God Cannot Be Defined

Some Challenges

Distractions Away from God

Science is Good – But not …

'Prove God'

Old-Age and the Terminally Ill

Bad Outcomes Resulting from Science

Hate and Evil Today in the Name of God

Some Positive Shared Messages

Free Will

Don't Blame God

Suffering, Us and God

Forgiveness

All are Equal in God's Eyes

The solution is Love – God's Love

Methods to Help Discover God

Social Media Solution for Injustice –
    IT Savvy Young

Philanthropy – A Wonderful
    Endeavour

God Loves Science

God Love the Wilderness

God Loves Beauty

God Loves Humour

God's Simple Messages - Summary

Conclusion

Appendix 1   Revelation from God
    Mt Warning

Appendix 2   Personal Notes After
    Revelation

Bibliography

Index

Reviews

'GOD Today' Series

Websites by Author and Publisher

Background Stories by Author

Story 1	25th Birthday Life Changer
Story 2	Year 11
Story 3	Nimbin – Alternative Lifestyle
Story 4	Cyclonic Surf Near Drownin
Story 5	"Let Go and Let God"
Story 6	Employment Selection & God
Story 7	Saudi Arabia - Islam and God
Story 8	God in Nature – Australia Trip
Story 9	Uluru/Ayers Rock Sunset
Story 10	Ubirr, Kakadu National Park
Story 11	Niagara Falls, Canada/USA
Story 12	When in Rome, Italy

Story 13	Deconsecrated Christ Church Cathedral, New Zealand & Earthquake
Story 14	St Patrick's Cathedral, New York, USA and St Paul's Cathedral, London, UK.
Story 15	Zojoji (Buddhist) Temple, Tokyo, Japan
Story 16	Gold Coast – Australia's Tourist Capital - Home
Story 17	Surfing with the Dolphins
Story 18	Mt Warning - Word of God
Story 19	Colleague's Wedding – 'Let Go and Let God'
Story 20	Share the Bounty
Story 21	*Rosies: Friends on the Street*
Story 22	God in the Marginalised – The Indigenous
Story 23	Compassionate Wealthy Help Humanity
Story 24	God Must be Seen as Central in the Religious School

Story 25   The Catholic School is Seen as Church

Story 26   The Arts and the Creator God - Louvre, Paris, France & Vatican Museum, Italy Highlighted

Appendix 7

'Where's God? Revelations Today'

(Book 3 in 'GOD Today' Series)

CONTENTS

Foreword by Karen Foster

Preface

'GOD Today' Series

Introduction

Author

Keep It Simple

PART 1

GOD'S REVELATION

Introduction to Part 1

Revelations and Inspired Messages from God

Are the Revelations and Messages contained in this book the Truth from God?

Tears from God

Free Will

God's Revelation

Mt Warning – Word of God Revelation – the Story

God's 12 Revelations

> Rev #1 - 'Be truthful'
>
> Rev #2 – 'Don't be greedy'
>
> Rev #3 – 'Love life – don't take it'
>
> Rev #4 – 'Respect all'
>
> Rev #5 – Love one another as I have loved You
>
> Rev #6 – Be educated for what is right and Truthful
>
> Rev #7 – Education is paramount for all
>
> Rev #8 – We are one
>
> Rev #9 – One God only – One God

One God. One Name.

No one religion

…strengthens personal religious belief

What the major world religions … say…

Religious Scripture Commentators' Views

Rev #10 – God's messages to a world in need

Rev #11 – This world is in enormous need

Rev #12 – Fear rules – often from the cyber world – eliminate this

Revelation Notes

God's Prior Afternoon Inspirations

Inspired Message #1 – God sits with permanent tears in God's eyes

Inspired Message #2 – Not the warrior image

Inspired Message #3 – But the loving, caring, for all others…

Inspired Message #4 – The body truly is the Temple of God

Inspired Message #5 – Purify it   1

Inspired Message #6 – Don't harm, poison it…illicit drugs,   smoking.

Where it all began – Author's 25th birthday

PART 2 UNDERSTANDING GOD

Introduction to Part 2

God

    We NEED GOD!

    Why Believe in God?

    Some Different Reasons

        Sun & Signs

        Unique Sun Formations

Sun Arrows – Head and Heart

Coincidence and God's Messages

God Cannot Be Defined

Love

God Loves You

But - Life's Not Fair

You Can't Have Everything

All are Equal in God's Eyes

Our Divine Eyes

The Solution is God's Love

Forgiveness

Life & Death

Each Day is a Bonus from God

Truly Alive

Going Home… to God

Heaven – What's It Like?

Science

    God and Science – Science is Good

    Bad Science Possibilities

Suffering

    The Mystery of Suffering

    Suffering, Us and God

Major World Changes Needed

    Two Reformations Needed – Secular and Islamic

    Major Challenges to Western World

    Islamic Reformation. Islam Must Reject All Violence

God's Other Inspired Messages

Conclusion

Appendix 1 *1God.world: One God for All* – Content

Appendix 2 Revelation to Dissemination personal challenges

Bibliography

Index

Reviews for Book 1: '1God.world: One God for All'

Websites' details

Appendix 8

'Where's God? Revelations Today Photobook Companion: GOD Signs (2nd ed)'

(Book 4 in 'GOD Today' Series)

Outstanding and Unique sun and cloud images, mostly with the author actually receiving sun arrows, etc.

These need to be seen to believe it!

Author's Favourite Photobook.

Introduction

Foreword

Unique Sun Formations

Easter Sun Crosses

Sun Arrows and Flares

Unique Sun Formations – Authenticity

Straddie Sun Arrows + Double Rainbow

Mt Warning Cloud – Rays Shooting Outwards

Revelations and Inspired Messages from God

    Background

    Justification

God's Revelations #1-12

Head, Heart and Hands

Coincidence and God's Messages

The Magnificent Glorious Sun – Sunrises and Sunsets

    Canada

    Australia

Mt Warning

The Foot of Mt Warning

'GOD Today' Series

Author's Websites

Appendix 9 (Draft)

Love is the Meaning of Life: GOD'S Love

(Book 6 in 'GOD Today' Series)

To be released in 2020/1

CONTENTS
Foreword
'GOD Today' Series
Introduction
Author
What is love?
Love's Challenges
Love's Solutions
Love is the Meaning of Life – God's Love
Religious Challenges
Religious Solutions

Conclusion

Bibliography

Index

Author's Websites

Other Books by the Author

Appendix 10

Islam, Christianity, Secularism – Today's Key Challenges

'Jesus and Mahomad are God' highlight God's desire for the world's two largest religions to be thoughtfully and respectively challenged to become more wholesome and loving institutions and communities for their followers and others worldwide. And to include these latest two Revelations #6 and #15 in their teachings, etc. This is all about the genuine LOVE from God for each other, no matter religion, denomination or culture.

Islam and Christianity need to accept the challenges and move forward significantly. In this case, based on the Revelations and inspired messages, the author has received from God and explored in this *'God Today' Series* of seven/eight books.

It is now time for the followers of Islam to realise that no one is threatening them with these new additional Revelations and messages from God.

They will need to accept that it is not just very probable for God to do this but that God has done this!

In fact, not just very possible but well within the expectations of many of their followers no doubt. People of this world are calling out very loudly for Islam to accept more Revelation and inspired messages from God.

A 'Renaissance' and 'Reformation', similar to those that affected Christianity these past centuries, are seen to be needed by Islam. Such development will help them move forward into the present day. It is not wrong or anti-Islamic, anti–Allah, anti-Muhammad or anti-Qur'an etc., because it is from God's Revelations via a genuine modern-day teacher with a considerable academic, personal and professional background in these religious areas.

It is God's choice.

There is nothing wrong with this notion. God does not stay still. Neither must we. As the world grows, develops and changes very regularly these decades, so too must we be prepared for God's religious developments being genuine and necessary.

God/Allah calls Muslims through modern-day religious laypeople, one example being this book's author, to listen very carefully to the latest Revelations and messages from God. God has said these things in the urgency of hope to the Islamic followers of God.

Muslims are not being forced or coerced into anything they don't need, but they are being challenged to search out what it is that God commands from Islam and for Islam in today's world of continuous and significant changes. Allah/God is calling for Love, Peace and Acceptance of all genuine religions.

The number one idea is to promote worldwide theologically, that no more violence or death can be metered out by any religion or culture, especially in this case of fundamental religious followers from various faiths. Muslims must accept that taking significant steps forward and not living in the 6th century, or any other era up unto the present time is essential for a satisfied, happy and non-divided world – a world of love and not hate!!! A society existing for all people, of all faiths and cultures equally. A beautifully supported world from the one and only God forever! An exceptional existence will then be created for followers of Islam and all other religions who aim to benefit from these latest Revelations. Listen to the world of various religions and denominations. Hear what they say. Adapt this to your beliefs and actions. Be well-informed about the Qur'an and be accurate in disseminating its teachings. Don't exaggerate any teachings which males of the warrior age (i.e. the teens, twenties to thirties) would find incredibly enticing. Include these new Revelations discussed in this Book as being from God for all Muslims and Christians, and all other people living today. Quote the Qur'an honestly, without exaggeration or truth-stretching. Be open to the Truths stated by Allah/God.

Allah/God loves ALL people within this world now, previously and forever, equally! No matter their differences or to which religion each belongs. Genuinely following the one true God of all creation and of all time should be the aim of all religions today!!! God always loves us equally. It is we who choose to either not love God or various people.

Islamic followers grow into the massive new light that awaits you from Allah/God!!! The world is ready and wants you as part of its fully functioning and legitimate beliefs and practices to become one with all the other religions and cultures. Not to be fighting these other genuine religions and cultures.

The violent Islamic fundamentalists, e.g. ISIS, and all others who profess violence from any faith, along with individual secular groups and deniers of God, must STOP NOW!!! God demands!!!

It is violence against various groups, Islamic and otherwise, and subjugation of women's, children's and many disadvantaged rights, and all peoples' equality with men, which are some of the main disagreements. The extreme fundamentalist Muslims' violence against other

Muslims and their denominations, as well as other religions, is out of the misunderstood God who makes it very clear in all genuine religions that all people are equal no matter their financial 'successes', social standing, career, gender, religious leadership, etc. It is the people who turn away from God through their sinning, not God turning away from the people. God never turns from people – because God is absolute LOVE.

The vast majority of peaceful Muslims and their leaders, along with our political world leaders, must stop the violent followers of Islam (and any other violently passionate religious people from any other religion). It is a difficult task, yet an essential one for world peace. It is something everyone needs to support and act on in their own best ways.

There is only ONE GOD for all religions, for all cultures, for all genders, overall times! The One God appeared to various cultures, whenever God wanted to, for whatever reason God wanted, whenever God wanted to do so.

No-one or religion has any right to claim God as their own and ignore everyone else! God, the one and only, is for everyone in whatever way God desires. For all genuine religions, God is the only God – forever, past, present and future. If this is still not how God is seen, then it is their duty and obligation to change now at God's instruction. This Revelation, to us, all should have a significant impact on all religions worldwide. No one's God is better than anyone else's because there is only one God for eternity. There is no competition. There is the only *ONE GOD* for everyone, forever. (There are not multiple god's for each religion, just the one and only God of all time.)

The secular world and those following secular philosophies are being urgently called by God to once again refocus on God and God's supporting Revelations. Don't be ruled by fools-gold – be ruled by the absolutely ONE and ONLY God…

Just as Islam needs some radical changes and development to move successfully into a modern-day Islam, so do many of those predominantly coming from western-secular societies.

Their God of importance worth following is a heretical stance by these secularists. It is also evil! Choosing anything but God and moving voluntarily away from God is evil! Yes, everyone has the personal option to believe and follow God. Free Will is essential for loving choices – no force, pressure, bullying, etc.

Those who know very little about God and live their lives in kind, considerate and loving ways, and do not reject our only God whom they don't know about, are innocent in God's eyes.

However, those who do know of God and have various genuine beliefs about God, but yet are denying God, are genuinely evil and moving away from God while on Earth. Their choice at death would most likely be a continuation of their earthly lifestyle, i.e. moving towards or being at, the evil state of existence. This would then progress in death as in life – a permanent evil presence and not a Heavenly, loving one unless the person sort genuine, authentic forgiveness from God and was truly sorry for all the evil caused in this person's life.

But it falls upon key religious people in all religions, to make a case for believing and following God while including these twenty-one latest Revelations, as essential beliefs needed to be espoused, understood, appreciated, implemented and followed significantly as the Truth.

Appendix 11

'OMG' – 'Oh, My God!' Little Respect for God?

Help or Hindrance?

This 'OMG' is one response continually used by westerners for moments when being startled, shocked, loved, challenged positively or negatively, etc. But why?

 "Our prayers are for those affected adversely by the recent flood!" Then it all changed, and many wonder if God has taken a 'back seat' or was forced out of everyday life by atheists, agnostics, or the other doubting, questioning, unsure ones of our world.

The OMG has just become a commonly used call, used by people needing or acknowledging the help required or acknowledging extraordinary good or bad experiences.

One could ask, why do western civilisations continually throw one-liners about God around? Knowing it is just a phrase used to place themselves somehow in the middle of a trendy/cool response group. To be seen as cool and one with the cool guys! But not with the divine they are calling out to when using OMG, etc.

Most other cultures and religions of the Middle East, Asia, Africa and the Oceania, etc. would see this western 'cry' as an insult to God and those followers of God. These religions and cultures can't understand how other cultures and faiths can respond to what is often considered as a heretical call to God, an insult to God and an insult to genuine followers of God!

These statements are thrown around by the young, adolescent and young adults mostly, but not only. Each is also commonly used by slightly older 'cool' people wanting to be seen as certain types of people within their social, family, career, etc. groups.

OMG!!! It's time to acknowledge that this habit of calling out' OMG' or saying 'Oh My God' is just a weak response to something affecting the respondent. It isn't cool or acceptable, whether these people think so or not!

It is an insult of God for thinking people because God wasn't most likely the recipient of its call and people were saying it for simplistic reasons. It was not associated with God or God's divinity and unbelievable powerfulness to help all people out as needed equally over their lifetimes.

> OMG!!! It's time to acknowledge that this common and growing habit of responding with 'OMG' or 'Oh My God' is mostly just a weak or ignorant response to something affecting the respondent… where's God in this?
>
> It is actually an insult to God from people, because God wasn't most likely the recipient of its call…

God should always be mentioned with absolute respect!!!

God's divinity and position to help all people out as needed equally over their lifetimes, must be priority #1.

Appendix 12 (Cont. from p33)

Atheists and Agnostics

Yes, we all have Free Will and [hopefully Informed] Consciences; however, at this stage, rejector atheists are being called out, because theirs is not a loving movement but an evil one! Blaming God for anything and everything that seems to go wrong is vindictive. *Humanity and individuals are the ones who freely do evil acts – God never does.* Yet, there are usually enough incidents to make various people question God's place unfairly. However, *the Love of God, which has been given to us all equally, should be used by the rejectors and the believers alike to find the real Truth about God.* But we should absolutely never give up on you. Trying to bring the lost to be the found is one of the greatest gifts of all from God for the non-believer and us faithful together!

Non-believers or Agnostics

Non-believers and agnostics who aren't sure if there is a God should be on the permanent move to find God! As opposed to doing nothing and going nowhere near God, for whatever reason.

To use every available means provided by this world and its loving individuals and populations for the answers needed to help select God as GOD! Yes, everyone has a right to their beliefs. But everyone needs to find God and bring God closely into their lives.

The vast majority of humanity are believers and will stay that way for their whole lives. Most of these believers will remain quiet, believing religion/spirituality is personal. They won't get dragged into uncomfortable debates, etc. Is it possible for this present time that responders who disagree, or wish to challenge the contents in this Book 5, be not so evil, hateful, and destructive? My social media religious experience would profoundly challenge this desire for the loving peace from God coming from the atheists and non-believers.

Yet, I would very much welcome these people to be open to offering their thoughts and beliefs, respectively, and listening carefully to the other side – the believers. This book is not provided as an opportunity to try and convince God believers to become non-believers. It is an offer for them to listen for the Truth about God's existence and to explore relevant topics. This isn't debatable in the vindictive way shown to me previously. But as a crutch to find genuine, awesome Godly facts and emotions. Don't forget how this works…

God wins!!! Evil eventually loses out!

GOD IS REAL NO MATTER WHAT!!!

Bibliography

Primary source
GOD

Secondary Sources
Books and Videos

Ali, Ayaan Hirsi, (2016), *Heretic: Why Islam Needs a Reformation Now*, Harper Collins, New York.

Foster, B., *1God.world: One God for All*, 2016, Great Developments Publishers, Gold Coast.

Foster, B., *Where's God? Revelations Today,* 2018, Great Developments Publishers, Gold Coast.

Foster, B., *Where's God? Revelations Today Photobook Companion: GOD'S Signs,* 2018, Great Developments Publishers, Gold Coast.

Foster, B., *Love is the Meaning of Life: GOD'S Love (2nd ed)*, 2020, Great Developments Publishers, Gold Coast. (Draft)

Foster, B., YouTube videos commenced in 2009 – efozz1 (780+ free videos)

Websites

Websites viewed in 2020 unless otherwise stated.

https://www.amazon.com/Bryan-Foster/e/B005DOPRMO%3Fref=dbs_a_mng_rwt_scns_share

An Introduction to Discernment
https://plenarycouncil.catholic.org.au/listening-and-discernment/

Bartunek, Fr J., 2015, What is the Gift of Tears'?'
https://spiritualdirection.com/2015/01/26/what-is-the-gift-of-tears

Brahman - Gods or goddesses
https://www.bbc.co.uk/religion/religions/hinduism/beliefs/intro_1.shtml

https://www.bbc.co.uk/religion/religions/buddhism/ataglance/glance.shtml (17/11/2009)

Coronavirus vaccine: Everything you need to know, https://www.medicalnewstoday.com/articles/coronavirus-vaccine

Crusades, Christianity https://www.britannica.com/event/Crusades

Fenelong, M, (2016) *Receiving the 'gift of tears'* in Our Sunday Visitor, https://osvnews.com/2016/08/23/receiving-the-gift-of-tears/

http://www.greatdevelopmentspublishers.com/ - Publisher's new webpage. (Original website started in 2007, closed 12/2018.)

https://www.facebook.com/groups/38960269805142 6/ - 1God.world Facebook

https://au.linkedin.com/in/bryanfoster

https://twitter.com/1Godworld1 - Twitter

https://www.instagram.com/ - Instagram (1godworld)

Foster, B., https://www.bryanfosterauthor.com/

Foster, B., https://www.godtodayseries.com/

Foster, B., https://www.JesusandMahomadareGod.com/

GCSE BBC, http://www.bbc.co.uk/schools/gcsebitesize/rs/god/chrevelationrev1.shtml

God Today, Facebook Group https://www.facebook.com/groups/389602698051426/

https://www.ncronline.org/blogs/peace-pulpit/everyday-prophets-are-our-midst (2020)

Islam: Truth or Myth? https://www.bible.ca/islam/islam-history.htm

Judaism and Numbers https://www.myjewishlearning.com/article/judaism-numbers/

Oxford Scholarship Online, Jesus the Fullness of Revelation, http://www.oxfordscholarship.com/view/10.1093/acprof:oso/9780199605569.001.0001/acprof-9780199605569-chapter-5

Rattner, R, The Emotion of Devotion – Crying for God, https://sillysutras.com/the-emotion-devotion-crying-for-god/

Taylor, F, (2016), Life after death: What did Jesus do between his resurrection and ascension? https://www.christiantoday.com/article/life.after.death.what.did.jesus.do.between.his.resurrection.and.ascension/82998.htm

'Tears from God…' video at https://www.youtube.com/watch?v=z5mmNvIKko4

The Everyday Prophets are in Our Midst https://www.ncronline.org/blogs/peace-pulpit/everyday-prophets-are-our-midst

What is the significance of the number 40 in Judaism? https://www.quora.com/What-is-the-significance-of-the-number-40-in-Judaism

What is the Significance of Number Forty in Islam? https://salamislam.com/lifestyle/what-significance-number-forty-islam.

Note
Bibliographic References Variation

When searching the Bibliography or in-text references for specific research background details, you will observe the standard intext and bibliographic styles. You will also discover what I refer to as the Primary Revelation References, which is directly from God to me. This is stated at the beginning of the Bibliography.

> **Bibliography**
>
> Primary source
>
> **GOD**

The primary reference for this book, *Jesus and Mahomad are GOD* and its series, *'GOD Today' Series,* is considerably different and unique from most other publications available worldwide today.

The Primary Revelation References are Revelations directly from God to me. These are not referenced from worldly publications, due to their nature and not being of this world's physical creation, but from the divine source. Each is as taken from God unless the details are stated otherwise.

It is the principal style used in Books 1, 3 and 5. Each reference becomes quite apparent in the various book articles, explanations and details. These may be direct Revelations from God or Inspired Messages from God or other forms of discerned vital points from God.

As an example, let us consider the 21 Revelations, including Revelation #15, which is the title of this book, *Jesus and Mahomad are God*. Each of these 21 Revelations is directly from God and recorded by me on three separate occasions, 1982, 2016 and 2018. The explanations of each have been discerned from God over the years. These were either as Inspired Messages or key discerned vital points.

Revelations appear to be 'spoken' by God, while Inspired Messages are 'felt/experienced' as from

God. Vital points are primarily discerned and experienced as being known to be the Truth from God and significantly add to the details being inspired by God. These are more daily information from God. These complete the necessary detail for appreciating God's specific points, messages and Revelations.

The Secondary References are as expected and as used by most everyday readers and academics. This is both for in-text referencing and the bibliography.

Revelations appear to be 'spoken' by God, while Inspired Messages are 'felt/experienced' as from God. Vital points are primarily discerned and experienced as being known to be the Truth from God and significantly add to the details being inspired by God. These are more daily information from God.

Revelations appear to be 'spoken' by God, while

Inspired Messages are 'felt/experienced' as from God.

Vital points are primarily discerned and experienced, as being known to be the Truth from God and significantly add to the details being inspired by God. These are more like 'daily information' from God.

Index

1, 275, 300, 301, 304, 309
1 God, 300, 301, 309
1God.world, 21, 23, 61, 63, 126, 269, 312, 313, 336
Absolute Love, 67
acting, 7
Arts, 306
Australia, 7, 12, 118, 273, 304, 305
Australian, 119, 272
Ayers Rock, 304
background, 272
Belief, 301
Believe, 300, 310
Buddhist, 305
Canada, 304
caravan, 272
Cathedral, 305
Catholic, 276, 293, 306
challenge, 128, 275
challenges, 114, 121, 295, 297
challenging, 67, 114, 297
charismatic, 293, 294, 295
Christ, 305
Christianity, 119, 125, 128, 266
Church, 305, 306
communities, 107, 109
community, 105
COVID-19, 16, 149, **151**
culture, 107, 109
death, 252
Dedication, 13
divine, 275

educated, 107, 109, 205
emotion, 125
emotionally, 124
environment, 252
equally, 66
Evil, 302
faith, 292, 297
family, 273
Fear, 247, 250, 309
Forgiveness, 312
France, 306
Free Will, 302
freeing, 296
God, 16, 19, 21, 22, 23, 61, 63, 64, 65, 66, 67, 80, 104, 105, 107, 108, 110, 111, 112, 113, 114, 116, 117, 118, 119, 121, 122, 124, 125, 126, 127, 128, 129, 130, 131, 209, 210, 211, 265, 266, 267, 268, 269, 270, 272, 274, 275, 276, 292, 293, 294, 296, 297, 298, 299, 307, 308, 309, 310, 311, 312
God's Love, 302, 311
God's presence, 129
Gold Coast, 7, 305
health, 7
Heaven, 66, 311
history, 107, 109, 114, 274, 299
human, 114, 120, 209, 210
images, 64, 67, 112, 118, 249
Indigenous, 305
individual, 7, 105

individualistic, 107, 109
inherent, 125
inspiration, 126
inspired, 21, 63, 64, 80, 105, 110, 111, 113, 116, 126, 265, 266, 267, 269, 277
inspired messages, 16, 21, 63, 64, 80, 110, 111, 113, 116, 126, 265, 266, 267, 269
Inspired Messages, 265, 307
institutions, 107, 109, 252
Islam, 304
IT, 303
Italy, 304, 306
journey, 292
Kakadu, 304
Karen Foster, 13
Keep It Simple, 108, 307
KIS, 300
law, 12
life, 12, 108, 114, 121, 126, 130, 205, 250, 270, 292, 296, 308
Life, 62, 66, 67, 69, 311
Lifestyle, 304
London, 305
love, 12, 104, 292, 296, 297, 299
Love, 62, 66, 67, 68, 308, 311
loved, 205
loves, 66, 298
loving, 277
Mahomad, 160
meditation, 112, 119, 121

messages, 21, 63, 64, 104, 105, 107, 110, 122, 123, 126, 205, 265, 266, 268, 270, 309
Messages, 249, 308, 311
Mt Warning, 61, 63, 65, 112, 116, 117, 126, 127, 272, 274, 303, 305, 308
natural, 209, 266
New York, 305
New Zealand, 305
Niagara Falls, 304
Nimbin, 304
one, 107, 109, 127, 205, 274
One God, 21, 23, 61, 63, 126, 269, 308, 312, 313
oneness, 272, 292
Paris, 306
person, 295
Philanthropy, 303
population, 65
practices, 107
pray, 294, 296
prayer, 108, 112, 119, 121, 126, 295
presence, 126, 274, 275
principal, 294
Prophet, 16, 29, 44, 133
Qur'an, 130
Reformation, 312
Reformations, 312
religion, 104, 105, 107
religions, 107, 274
religious, 112, 114, 115, 118, 120, 252, 265, 267, 268, 275, 294, 309

Revelation, 19, 61, 63, 113, 116, 117, 126, 247, 266, 267, 269, 272, 275, 308, 309, 312, 337
Revelations, 16, 21, 22, 23, 61, 63, 64, 80, 107, 110, 111, 112, 116, 123, 126, 128, 163, 265, 267, 269, 270, 271, 276, 307, 308
Rome, 304
Rosies, 305
Saudi Arabia, 304
school, 276, 292, 293
Science, 302, 312
scripture, 130
sign, 117, 128, 130, 275, 297
simple, 105, 106, 108
sky, 65
societies, 107, 109
spiritual, 292, 294
spiritually, 124
stories, 23, 63, 269
story, 63, 116, 117, 126
Story, 301, 304, 305, 306
Stradbroke, 65, 117
Straddie, 65, 117
students, 293, 294
sun, 64
teachers, 105, 294, 296
tears, 124, 125, 126, 127, 275, 276, 277, 292, 296, 297, 299
Tears from God, 16, 112, 114, 115, 116, 123, 124, 125, 126, 127, 128, 130, 131, 265, 269, 275, 292, 297, 308, 338
theologians, 105
theological, 104
theology, 104
Tokyo, 305
truth, 295
Truth, 274
truthful, 205
twelve, 64, 119
Ubirr, 304
Uluru, 12, 304
USA, 7, 304, 305
Vatican, 306
western, 298
Western World, 312
Word, 272, 305
world, 21, 64, 65, 67, 104, 107, 109, 110, 114, 125, 209, 248, 250, 251, 252, 266, 268, 270, 298, 309
world today, 298

Author's Websites

https://www.godtodayseries.com/ - The main website for this series, includes the blog commenced in 2016

http://jesusandmahomadaregod.com/ - Book 5's website

https://www.bryanfosterauthor.com/ Author's website

http://www.greatdevelopmentspublishers.com/ - incl. Publisher's new webpage. (Original website started in 2007, ended 12/2018.)

https://www.facebook.com/groups/38960269805146/ - God Today, Facebook

https://au.linkedin.com/in/bryanfoster - LinkedIn

https://www.youtube.com/user/efozz1 - 780+ Free YouTube videos commenced in 2009

https://twitter.com/1Godworld1 - Twitter – being developed

https://www.instagram.com/ - Instagram (1godworld) – being developed

Release Dates for Revelations #1-21. 2016-2021.

#10 published in 2016 in

1God.world: One God for All

#1-12 published in 2018 in

Where's God? Revelations Today

#13-15 and #16-21 published in 2020 in

Jesus and Mohamad are God

Bryan Foster

Jesus and Mahomad are GOD

21 Revelations from God for Today's World

Bryan Foster

Published by:

Great Developments Publishers

Gold Coast, Australia

Bryan Foster and Karen Foster - Directors

Copyright © 2008 - 2020 Great Developments Publishers

Available

Books available from all good internet bookstores and various local bookshops and libraries.

e-books are available from Amazon, Apple and Blurb

(except Book 2 photobook from Apple and Blurb only)

BOOKS BY AUTHOR

Books - Out Now

1God.world: One God for All, (Author Articles) (2016)

Mt Warning God's Revelation: Photobook Companion to '1God.world', (2017) (available at Apple & Blurb.com only)

Where's God? Revelations Today, (Author Articles) (2018)

Where's God? Revelations Today Photobook Companion: GOD Signs (2nded) **(Spectacular, challenging, unique images from God.) (2018) **Author's favourite**.

Jesus and Mahomad are GOD (Author Articles) (2020)

Photobooks - Out Now

'God Today' Series' Images by Bryan Foster and Karen Foster, supported by Andrew Foster (Austographer.com)

'Straddie' North Stradbroke Island: Photobook of Natural & Shared Beauty, (2019)

Mt Warning Wollumbin Circuit: a photographic journey, (2018)

My Australia Photobooks Series – 10 x photobooks of Northern Territory and (FNQ) Far North Queensland, (2014-5) Bryan and Karen Foster

Marketing Books – School and Church - Out Now

School Marketing Manual for the Digital Age (3rd ed), (2008-1st, 2009-2nd, 2011-3rd)

Church Marketing Manual for the Digital Age (2nd ed), (2009-1st, 2011-2nd)

Books Coming

Love is the Meaning of Life: GOD'S Love (2nded) (Author Articles) (appr. late 2020)

Love is the Meaning of Life (1sted) (Author Articles) (appr. 2020/1)

Wisdom made real: A lifetime of Godly hints and tips for us all (Author Articles) (appr. 2021/2) (Working Title)

Most photobooks created from our travels around Australia.

Jesus and Mahomad are GOD

Bryan Foster

www.ingramcontent.com/pod-product-compliance
Lightning Source LLC
Chambersburg PA
CBHW050614300426
44112CB00012B/1498